to be made well

"Amy Julia Becker is one of the best practical theologians writing today. Her books are poignant, personal, and deeply profound, and *To Be Made Well* is no exception. Healing is a complex and complicated topic, but Amy Julia treats it with all the tender nuance and care it requires while offering hard-won insights along the way. If you are tired of simplistic answers but still searching for hope, you will find it here."

—**Sharon Hodde Miller**, author of *Free of Me: Why Life Is Better When It's Not about You*

"Amy Julia Becker is a brilliant writer who has masterfully explored the complex and sensitive topic of healing in a vulnerable, sobering, and comprehensive way. Whether sickness is in our body, our soul, or society, whether we are presently ill, recovering from illness, or on the way to being ill—this book will better equip you both for your journey in the healing process and to be an agent of healing."

—**David M. Bailey**, founder of Arrabon and coauthor of *A People, a Place, and a Just Society*

"Timely, practical, and full of hope, *To Be Made Well* is a beautiful offering for our weary, splintered, and hurting world. Amy Julia Becker skillfully addresses our personal and collective need for healing through examples from the Bible, from her own life, and from a diverse range of trusted leaders. These pages hold timeless lessons and helpful application. Highly recommend!"

—**Vivian Mabuni**, speaker, author of *Open Hands, Willing Heart*, and founder and podcast host of *Someday Is Here* for AAPI women leaders

"Amy Julia Becker has written a beautiful book, grounded in the person of Jesus and the healing he brings. This is not a book with a before-and-after story of miraculous healing; it is a book about how we live in a fractured world with bodies that bear on and in them the brokenness of living. It is a book about how we see Jesus, how he sees us, and how his love heals us just a little bit more each day."

—**Lore Ferguson Wilbert**, author of *A Curious Life: The Questions God Asks, We Ask, and We Wish Someone Would Ask Us* and *Handle with Care: How Jesus Redeems the Power of Touch in Life and Ministry*

"In an age marked by division, detachment, and dis-ease at every level, from the intimately personal to our society at large, Amy Julia Becker has a word of hope: Jesus can make us whole and well. What that holistic healing looks like and how we can participate in it is the creative gift offered in these pages."

—**David Swanson**, pastor of New Community Covenant Church and CEO of New Community Outreach

"Amy Julia Becker's words have been a salve for my soul for many years, and the words in this book are no different. With vulnerability, wisdom, and grace, Amy Julia guides us towards seeking and understanding what it really means to be made well. I hope everyone reads this book."

—**Heather Avis**, *New York Times* bestselling author of *The Lucky Few* and *Different: A Great Thing to Be*

"Amy Julia Becker turns the stories of the bleeding woman and Jairus's daughter over like a prism to show readers all facets and shed light on our personal, spiritual, and communal longings to be whole. Her writing is honest, insightful, and unafraid of complexity, always leading us beyond ourselves and into the mystery of Jesus, our ultimate healer. I hope many read this book and accept the invitation to participate in God's deep and wide work of healing."

—**Liuan Huska**, author of *Hurting Yet Whole: Reconciling Body and Spirit in Chronic Pain and Illness*

to be made well

an **INVITATION** *to* **WHOLENESS,**
HEALING, *and* **HOPE**

AMY JULIA BECKER

HERALD
PRESS

Harrisonburg, Virginia

Herald Press
PO Box 866, Harrisonburg, Virginia 22803
www.HeraldPress.com

Study guides are available for many Herald Press titles at www.HeraldPress.com.

TO BE MADE WELL
© 2022 by Herald Press, Harrisonburg, Virginia 22803. 800-245-7894.
    All rights reserved.
Library of Congress Control Number: 2021058457
International Standard Book Number: 978-1-5138-0971-7 (paperback);
    978-1-5138-0973-1 (ebook); 978-1-5138-0972-4 (hardback)
Printed in United States of America

26 25 24 23 22   10 9 8 7 6 5 4 3 2 1

Contents

Foreword

As I lay dying in a hospital bed at twenty-six years old . . . As I sit across the table from a mom devastated by the grief of her story . . .

As I read the article crying out for justice after unimaginable loss . . .

The question is always the same.

Will I be healed? Will we be healed?

And then a deeper question remains—what does *healing* even mean?

This may be the ultimate struggle of our humanity. Knowing we have this glorious welling up of great possibility in us, of golden dreams, but finding it all, more often than not, just out of our reach.

We are wounded. We are disabled. We are in pain. We are grieving. We are lost.

And the juxtaposition between what could be but is not yet and may never be is almost too much to bear.

On an ordinary day in April 2008, I suffered a catastrophic and nearly fatal stroke, completely out of the blue as my six-month-old baby napped and my husband finished his final law school presentation in the next room. Our lives were upended in a moment. And my near lifeless body lay in an ICU bed on life support for months afterward.

A beautiful community of friends and family and internet strangers prayed and loved us through that terrible season. From around the world, visions and dreams of me bounding out of the hospital like a modern-day Jairus's daughter, resurrected from the dead, began to flow to our inboxes and hearts. Healing would come. Everyone was hoping and praying and believing it would be so.

And yet months later, I could barely breathe or move on my own, much less run back into the world as if nothing had happened. The dreams of healing from our community and in our own hearts began to fade. The grief of unanswered prayers was perhaps the deepest we have ever experienced.

As time passed, I gradually got better and better—more of a "slow motion miracle" than the instantaneous type— and I did desire to share my story, telling people about how Jesus had healed me. But I certainly didn't plan to tell it from a wheelchair.

Yet as many more years of recovery passed and significant disabilities remained, it became clear that no amount of prayers or tears or magical cures would restore the part of my brain that had been removed to save my life. This second chance would include a wheelchair and would look nothing like the life I had imagined living.

But then there were the stories. Over years of meeting people living through similarly unresolved questions, of hearing stories of disability and trauma and hope, our hearts opened to the possibility of redefining healing. And stories, like the one Amy Julia Becker has lived and told, helped us reimagine everything.

In a season when we longed to know we were not alone in the unique isolation and wounding of disability, her book *A Good and Perfect Gift* opened our eyes to the gift of the life and the miracle right in front of us.

White Picket Fences poignantly put words around my similar longings to steward my privilege and hurts for the cause of my co-sufferers.

And now this book, *To Be Made Well*—which may be my favorite yet—draws on all these separate but interconnected themes. This book is as personal as it is universal. It has not been formed theoretically from pages in libraries; rather, it has been lived out and embodied in community.

This is a guidebook full of hard-earned insight. This is a trail blazed through the wilderness.

If my own story of longing for healing and finding hope in the process has taught me anything, it's that this lifelong journey of heart-breaking and remaking is most powerfully done together.

My story of disability has offered a bigger reality that none of us can do this life alone, nor were we meant to. We need God, and we need each other. And in this universal longing for healing, we can't find what we're looking for alone either. Nor were we meant to.

I'm so grateful for Amy Julia's vulnerable and wise offering in these pages. It may just be the beginning of your own redefining.

May the places of our deepest wounding eventually also be the places of our deepest healing. May that healing come in ways we never imagined. May the upending of our lives help us better see the upside-down kingdom of God. And may we all be made well, together.

—Katherine Wolf
Founder of Hope Heals and author
of *Hope Heals* and *Suffer Strong*

Introduction

I started throwing up when I was fourteen years old. It began on a Friday night in December, a few hours after our family of six enjoyed a special dinner in the restaurant of a local hotel. The lobby looked festive, with white lights and greenery and holiday music in the background. A magician moved from table to table, hiding coins and pulling scarves out of unexpected crevices. My little sisters giggled with delight.

It came time to order dinner, and I faced a decision. I hadn't eaten a full meal in weeks. Earlier that fall, I had vowed to limit myself to one thousand calories per day. I wrote this goal in my journal and signed it, a pledge to myself and to the gods of thinness.

I had just come home from fall term at a boarding school, so my mother wasn't aware of my dramatic shift in eating. She would have registered concern about my new diet of apples, frozen yogurt, bagels, and salad. That night, I broke my pledge. I ordered fajitas and an ice cream sundae. I wanted the pretense of normalcy. I didn't want my family to notice that anything had changed.

The food tasted sumptuous, but I worried about what the scale would tell me in the morning. Once we returned to our house, I decided to balance out the meal by riding the stationary bike in our attic. My dad worked out twice a day, so even at the odd hour of nine at night, no one in my family thought much about my decision to exercise. The surprise came just before I got in the shower, when I threw up. I didn't feel nauseated. I didn't gag. It was more like a polite, unexpected, not even entirely unpleasant regurgitation. I mentioned it with a shrug to my mom the next morning. But then it happened again the next night. And the next. Within a few weeks, I was involuntarily regurgitating everything that went into my body.

In February, I was admitted to the hospital for observation. The plan was to feed me scrambled eggs with radioactive particles and then watch those eggs move through my digestive track. But the eggs didn't move. They sat in my gut.

"Your stomach walls look gray," my gastroenterologist said. "Like the stomach of a ninety-year-old." The technical diagnosis was *gastroparesis*. My stomach was paralyzed.

Identifying the cause of the problem didn't make a difference. I couldn't keep down any food. I was losing weight. I took medication to improve motility, but it didn't help. After a year of painful blood draws and tests and tubes that never amounted to much change in my condition, we tried acupuncture and biofeedback. I tried a diet restricted to simple, soft foods. I tried drinking only Ensure. I tried prayer—members of our church gathered around me, prayed for healing, and anointed me with oil. And Shirley Prey—an elder whose spiritual gifts fit her name—said to me gently after the anointing:

"This one will take a long time." I went on and off intravenous fluids, in and out of the hospital, became familiar with fainting from rising too fast. Those early months turned into five years of struggle.

A part of me wanted to get better, but mostly I felt relieved that I could eat without fear of what the scale would report, and relieved that I couldn't be blamed for self-harm. I had friends with anorexia and bulimia who were in and out of treatment centers and therapist offices. But I could tell myself, and my parents and teachers and doctors, that my body was inexplicably malfunctioning and I simply needed a medical cure.

Looking back decades later, I vacillate between calling this illness an eating disorder and accepting the medical diagnosis of gastroparesis. I can see my unhealthy mindset around food. But my body also was clearly impaired. I still don't have the words to combine the bodily and psychological reality. Pulling the threads of the physical and the emotional aspects of my situation only results in a tighter knot. Even now—when I think of how often as an adult I've succumbed to illness in a time of stress, or when I think of friends lying in bed from migraines while managing the pressure of childcare and working at home during a pandemic, or when I read about the increase in debilitating back pain and substance use disorders and anxiety in the modern era—I see in myself and in our culture an inability to connect the physical, emotional, spiritual, and social aspects of who we are. And I, like many others, feel a longing for that connection. A longing for healing.

Two years into my illness, my boyfriend at the time (and now my husband) confronted me. He had noticed how I excused myself from every meal. He noticed my dry, brittle hair and skinny limbs. He noticed my evasive answers to questions about food. He asked me to count how often I threw up in a day. The next night I told him: eight times.

Peter insisted I needed help, and I was both ashamed and relieved to agree with him. This time, I felt certain that the answers would come from uncovering my emotions around food and my body. So I went to therapy. I met with a nutritionist. I ate as she instructed, and I gained twenty pounds over the course of a few months. Until one day, I broke. I returned to the familiar pattern. Soon thereafter, I found myself in the emergency room. Routine bloodwork indicated my heart was in danger of stopping. I was seventeen years old.

As I saw it, doctors had failed me. Therapy and nutritionists had failed me. And prayer had failed me. I had wanted God to swoop in and offer an immediate and miraculous change to my body, and that didn't happen. All I had left was myself. Four years in, I set a goal of "only" throwing up twice each day. Then a goal of once a day. Then once every other day. It was miserable. I hated the changes to my body. I hated the sensation of forcing food into my stomach. But I also wanted to get well. I started to take small steps that seemed to actually make a difference. I stopped buying magazines like *Self* and *Shape* and *Glamour*, with images of women in bathing suits and promises of the next great food or exercise fad on their covers. I memorized Bible verses about how God cares about our hearts and not about the way our bodies look. And I started to receive physical therapy for my stomach.

Once a week, I lay on a table—passive, receptive—and talked as Kim, the physical therapist, pressed on my abdomen and kneaded my paralyzed organs back to life. She asked basic questions like "What's your favorite food?" When I talked about how much I loved french fries, my stomach audibly gurgled, as if the prospect of that nourishment and pleasure demanded a bodily response. For years, I had carefully separated the physical and mental aspects of my being, but telling Kim simple stories about my parents, my sisters, my boyfriend, my school, combined with her gentle massage, seemed to knit me back together. I could feel my stomach wake up. Over the course of a few months of weekly sessions, I finally began to get well.

I didn't have the language for it at the time, but I was learning that our modern medical system—as marvelous and innovative as it is—has tremendous limits when it comes to healing. I recognized this disconnect again in my mid-twenties when my mother-in-law was diagnosed with cancer and doctors could recommend treatments but didn't know how to offer care as she faced the reality of a terminal illness. I ran into it when our oldest daughter was diagnosed with Down syndrome and received labels of "defective" and "abnormal," as if who she was as a person could be reduced to a category called "disability." I saw it again in my thirties when my back began to hurt and I couldn't explain where the pain came from. And I needed this understanding when our nation entered a global pandemic and a time of racial reckoning, when a biomedical approach to healing was not enough to care for our wounded souls or our divided society.

Most people do not have such an extreme story of illness and disorder at such a young age. But all of us have been taught to isolate our bodies from our minds and our spirits. Many of us have physical ailments that stem from stress or heartache, whether it's the minor affliction of a cold sore on a lip or the major disruption of a chronic condition. And even when we do not carry our emotional pain within our own bodies, our bodies nevertheless feel the pain and division of the world around us.

We live in a society that assumes our personal and collective pain can be addressed through biomedical fixes. For Christians and other people of faith, we often hope for our own version of a "fix" through miraculous intervention. Sometimes surgeons or prayer can instigate immediate physical changes in our bodies. But even then, and especially when we wait and wait and wait without any change arriving—we are in need of a more comprehensive healing. As much as modern medicine can play a crucial role in our lives, it is nevertheless not enough to restore us—individually or collectively—to health. We need a broader and deeper understanding of healing in order to be made well.

This book is an exploration of this type of healing—comprehensive personal, spiritual, and communal restoration to a life-giving relationship with God. Looking at stories about Jesus, and especially the story of a synagogue leader and a bleeding woman in Mark's gospel, part 1 addresses the nature of Jesus' healing. This healing is for our whole selves—mind, body, and spirit. This healing is an invitation for each of us and all of us to know God's love personally. This healing is also a call to be received by and restored to community. Part 2 considers how distraction, shame, anxiety, and injustice can keep us from healing. And part 3 explores ways we are all invited to receive God's healing love, just as we are all invited to participate in extending that abundant love toward others.

My own longing for healing and wholeness began when I couldn't figure out a way to piece my body and soul together, when doctors, alternative medicine, therapists, and my own willpower didn't have the answers. Within all that confusion, I did turn to God. I didn't receive a quick fix, but I did receive a sense of God's presence. God was with me, even if my prayers weren't answered the way I thought they should be. I've now walked alongside others on their own journeys toward wholeness, and I have seen how healing can happen even in the midst of ongoing pain and unanswered questions. I now wonder whether God's refusal to cure my illness with a quick miracle was in and of itself an invitation to a deeper work of healing.

I emerged from those years of illness with a better understanding of how my body and mind and emotions were interrelated, with a deeper faith, and with a greater sense of purpose in the world. I was like the blind man healed by Jesus in John's gospel. Two thousand years later, I echoed his words, "I don't know who it was who healed me. I just know I once was blind and now I see."

PART I

The Nature of Healing

CHAPTER 1

Restored to Self

A woman was there who had been subject to bleeding for twelve years. She had suffered a great deal under the care of many doctors and had spent all she had, yet instead of getting better she grew worse. When she heard about Jesus, she came up behind him in the crowd and touched his cloak, because she thought, "If I just touch his clothes, I will be healed." Immediately her bleeding stopped and she felt in her body that she was freed from her suffering.

—MARK 5:25–29

When our kids were six, four, and one, we moved to a new town. My husband Peter had been hired as the head of an independent boarding school, and while I was still trying to write essays and blog posts and even books, I became more than ever the primary household manager and the "default" parent. Sometime within that first stressful year, my lower back began to ache.

During the day, I rarely noticed it. But at night, I woke up and squirmed as I fought to get comfortable. I tried exercises to strengthen my core. I tried stretching. I tried a pillow under my knees. Nothing really helped. I mostly overcame the pain and the accompanying sleeplessness with two Advil from the top drawer of the bathroom vanity, nestled alongside the hair-bands and nail clippers. Sometimes I included a Tylenol PM or melatonin in the cocktail of pain relief. Over the course of a few years, what had been intermittent pain became constant. The medication became a necessity.

The nightly Advil habit nagged at me. I didn't want to live the rest of my life popping pills in the dark. But then the pain began to creep toward my tailbone.

I told our daughter Marilee, four years old by this time, that I couldn't pick her up anymore, because it strained my back. I told William and Penny that it hurt me to have them sit on my lap. Those conversations brought with them both a sense of failure—I was supposed to be able to hold them close—and relief that I could reclaim a little bit of my sense of self. I didn't want to be blamed for having needs for things like time alone or personal space. I wanted instead to blame my body.

Stretching. Core strengthening. Medication. A self-pre-scribed Sisyphean regimen.

I finally reached out to a yoga teacher whom a friend rec-ommended. Maybe she could identify postural problems or guide my body into better balance or offer some stretches to practice every day. It seemed worth a try.

Anne is thin, strong, willowy, with long, straight, blonde hair. She wears cashmere cardigans and loose, flowy shirts atop leggings. She arrived at our back door with a gentle smile and a yoga mat. We walked upstairs together, and then she invited me with a gesture to sit cross-legged on the floor facing her. *This is going to hurt*, I thought. But I am nothing if not obedient to authority, so I took my uncomfortable seat.

She said, "Tell me why we're here."

I told her the story of my back trouble and all my attempts to cure the pain. I told her I thought I had a problem with alignment, and I wondered if she could help.

She nodded. "Whenever I hear the word *alignment*," she said, "I tend to think of what is out of balance in your life, not primarily in your body."

Regardless of whether she meant for me to do so, I took the prompt and spilled the story about the move three years earlier and Peter's job and my sense of failure as a writer and at home. There was the daily race against the clock, with Marilee at school for three hours each morning and dozens of doctor's visits for all of us and especially Penny, who rotates through a gauntlet of specialists who typically affirm her good health and suggest another appointment in six months' time. Then there was the role I played as wife of the head of school, whereby I showed up at parties and dinners and banquets and ceremonies and generally drank too much wine while trying to stay present and pleasant. There was the corresponding sense of losing myself—as the dial on the scale crept upward and the thought of a night without alcohol felt impossible.

It unraveled—this disjointed tale of what had started to feel like a meaningless existence. I was playing the role of supportive spouse and loving mother while the core of who I was had become so slippery it seemed in danger of sliding out of my grasp. Added to all that was the guilt of complaining about a life of wealth, safety, education, and relative health. The fear of not fulfilling my potential as a woman with an Ivy League education and a master's degree. The shame of not engaging with the real problems and injustices of the world because it all felt too big and overwhelming and I could hardly manage to take care of myself.

I talked about how even though I didn't like to admit it, I knew my back pain might be connected to all this emotional angst. By this time, I understood those years of gastroparesis and bulimia as a physical response to a set of emotional and psychological problems. Underneath my surface teenage desire to be as thin as possible were layers of disordered thinking—my need for control, my unwillingness to acknowledge any anger or hurt from family dysfunction, my belief that if I could only get everything right, then I would be lovable. Maybe something similar was happening now, in a subtler form, through this persistent back pain.

I sat cross-legged in the dim light of our hallway on a yoga mat, and I talked and talked and talked. We didn't move. For an hour, Anne asked questions that led me deeper into the story of my past and closer to admitting my discontent in the present. As I shared, it was as if the pain in my back had been stored up behind a valve that slowly opened and now allowed all that discomfort to seep out. Then, suddenly, my tailbone stopped hurting. At first, I didn't say it out loud. I didn't believe it could be true. But I hadn't felt this measure of relief in months, so as we neared the end of our session, I said, "I feel kind of bashful admitting this, but it seems to be all better now."

Anne nodded, as if this type of healing was as familiar to her as sunshine. "It doesn't usually happen this quickly," she said. "I think your experience in high school has helped you see the connection between your mind and your body."

"But I haven't figured it all out," I said. Feeling this kind of immediate relief didn't compute. I could see how the jumble of stories of my own self-doubt and identity loss was connected to this back pain. I also knew that talking about their reality hadn't changed anything about my situation as a wife, mother, or writer. I hadn't taken any steps to solve the problem. Nothing was fixed. Why would my back feel better so quickly?

"You don't need to figure it out for healing to begin. You just need to acknowledge the source of the pain," Anne said. "That pain will try to come back," she continued. "You need to develop a way to respond when it does. The lower back is the source of support for your whole body. So when you feel pain there, you can remind yourself, 'I am supported.'"

I couldn't make sense of it. But that morning I had experienced some sort of healing, and I wanted to continue on this healing path. So when I was steering our minivan down the windy road into town and my back started to throb, I repeated in my head, "I am supported." I envisioned the people who support me—Peter, friends, colleagues. And I turned those words of self-affirmation into a prayer, to the One who supports the cosmos itself and me within it.

I still had a lot of questions. Where did this healing come from? How did it work? Was personal healing just another form of self-help? Was it simply a sweet gift from God so I could feel better? Was there a larger purpose?

Healing began as something passive—when I was sitting with Anne and telling my story, I felt relief come upon me, like grace. Over time, when the pain crept back, I prayed through it. I began to ask God to help me understand what message my body was bringing when new aches and illnesses arose. Relief from pain was only the beginning. That moment also offered an invitation to explore shame and fear and loneliness. An invitation to experience wonder and delight and joy. An invitation to participate in a larger work of healing.

After that day with Anne, I began to read the Bible with new curiosity about Jesus as a healer. I turned to the stories in the Gospels, and as I did, I noticed the ubiquity of Jesus' healing work. On practically every page, someone gets healed. Often there's a sweeping statement about Jesus healing all the sick people who came to him on any given day. Mark writes about people running to Jesus wherever he went, pouring into the marketplaces of towns and villages and throughout the countryside, with sick and injured people carried on mats, desperate for healing (see Mark 6:55–56). When John the Baptist asks Jesus to prove whether he is the Messiah, the one sent by God to redeem Israel, Jesus tells John: "The blind receive sight, the lame walk, those who have leprosy are cleansed, the deaf hear, the dead are raised, and the good news is proclaimed to the poor" (Luke 7:22). To put it more succinctly, the way that Jesus both defines and defends his own ministry is by saying: "Healing, healing, healing, healing, healing, and some preaching. That's who I am. That's what I do. That's why I'm here."

At first glance, it can seem as though Jesus simply enacted the part of modern-day physician. He played the same role that Aleve or eyeglasses or orthopedic surgeons do now. Even as a Christian, for years I operated as though modern medicine had eliminated my need for Jesus' healing work. But to understand Jesus merely as an ancient doctor attending to physical woes is to miss the point.

When I look back on the way I approached both my stomach problems in high school and that lower back pain as an adult, I can see that I kept falling into two different misreadings of the Gospels that have shrunk many Christians' understanding of the nature of Jesus' healing. First, I followed the ancient Greek teacher Plato in splitting the soul from the body. In this way of thinking, the body is a breakable, woundable, limited shell. The soul is an eternal spirit filled with eternal possibilities. Early Christianity thrived in the Mediterranean world, and some of this Platonic division of body and soul trickled into Christian thought. For centuries since then, Christians like me have interpreted the New Testament scriptures as if they too divide body from spirit. We envisioned heaven as an ephemeral and abstract concept, a spiritual dimension alone. We made salvation into an insurance policy for the afterlife rather than an immediate transformation of life in the body here and now.

Second, I followed the thinkers from the Age of Enlightenment in Europe. Here, the material world, including our bodies, was factual and real. The spiritual was at best subjective and perhaps even illusory. As historian Brad Gregory puts it, for intellectuals in the Western world over the past few centuries, "to be a modern, educated person was necessarily to be without religious belief, because science reveals a natural world without God."[1] The Enlightenment led to tremendous advances in science and discovery, but it also led to a divorce between what became seen as two separate realms: the spiritual world (which was at best personal and perhaps imaginary) and the physical world (which was the world of reality).

But Jesus wasn't Greek, and Jesus wasn't European. As a Jewish man, he saw God's presence in and through all of creation, including human bodies. He understood the body and soul as integrally linked. And when he brought healing, it wasn't to the body and not the spirit or vice versa. He brought healing to the whole person.

As I began to try to understand my own experience of healing on a yoga mat on a Wednesday morning in September, I began to see how the biblical accounts of Jesus as a healer both subvert and challenge my Western understandings of healing. Many people are like me—we have lost sight of the connection between our minds and bodies. And many Christians are like me, too; we have lost sight of the fullness of the healing work

Jesus offers and invites us into—a healing that knits together body, mind, and spirit, a healing that connects the individual to the society, a healing that returns our whole selves to God.

That moment of relief from back pain gave me a newfound desire to understand what healing is, how it works, and why it matters. I returned again and again to one story from chapter 5 of Mark's gospel. The story begins with Jesus walking through a crowd. Soon, he is on his way to the house of a man named Jairus because Jairus, the local synagogue leader, has asked for his help. Jairus's daughter is desperately ill. It's a dramatic scene from the get-go—Jesus has been summoned to help a dying child, and a mass of people is headed with him toward her deathbed.

But then the attention shifts. We are introduced to a woman who has no name. A woman who has been bleeding for twelve years. A woman who is in pain. She has spent all her money looking for relief from doctors who have not been able to help her. She's the poorest of the poor, socially speaking. Not only is she without money, but her illness means she is ritually unclean and cannot worship in the temple in Jerusalem. She cannot touch other people without rendering them ritually unclean as well. She is alone in her suffering. She is desperate. But she also believes there may be hope for her. She sneaks up behind Jesus, touches the hem of his garment, and immediately feels that her bleeding has ceased.[2]

This moment so easily could be the end of the woman's story. She reaches out her hand. Her bleeding stops. Mission accomplished.

But Jesus doesn't see it this way. In fact, he stands still and asks, "Who touched me?"[3] His disciples point out the absurdity of his question—he is walking through a street thronged with people. But this woman knows that she is his answer.

She comes forward in fear. She wonders if he is calling her out because he is angry and wants to publicly shame her for stealing what did not belong to her. She—an unclean, outcast, destitute woman—has touched him, a holy religious teacher.

She wishes her encounter with Jesus were over. The disciples wish it were too. Jairus—a very important contact, a leader here in the community—has an urgent need for Jesus. There is no time to stop and talk. There is no time for the crowd. There is no time for this woman. There is important work to be done elsewhere. She is an interruption.

Mark writes that the woman told Jesus "the whole truth." And Jesus listened. We can only imagine what Jairus and the disciples thought about her story—Did they blame her for her illness? Did they scorn her for spending all her money on crackpot doctors? Did they feel compassion as they heard her talk? Or shame at having failed to care for her?

All we know is how Jesus responds: "Daughter, your faith has healed you. Go in peace and be freed from your suffering" (Mark 5:34).

In English, we can miss the richness of what Jesus wants for this woman, and the richness of what Jesus wants for us, because of the way we translate the Greek word for "healed." Our English translations come from the Greek word *sozo*. My Greek dictionary tells me that *sozo* means "save, rescue, deliver, keep safe, preserve, cure, make well."[4] The word our Bibles translate as "healed" could just as easily be translated "saved." *Your faith has healed you. Your faith has saved you.* Jesus' pronouncement is as much about spiritual transformation as it is about physical change.

There are two other Greek words that might have made more sense to use here. There's *iaomai*, which holds a simple meaning: "heal, cure, restore." And there's also *therapeuo*:

"heal, cure; serve."[5] The gospel writers employ these words elsewhere to talk about the immediate miraculous physical change that some people experience when they come to Jesus with sickness, disability, or pain. In this story, Mark initially tells us the woman has been cured, using the word *iaomai*, when we learn that her bleeding has stopped. But a few moments later, when she comes before Jesus, this other, more comprehensive word—*sozo*—comes into the story. When Jesus insists on meeting this woman face-to-face, he insists that more than curing has happened here.

In this encounter, Jesus calls forth her full humanity: mind, body, and spirit. She is not an object or a project but a woman being restored to herself, to her community, and to the God who loves her. In her encounter with Jesus, she has been saved, rescued, delivered, kept safe, preserved, cured, and made well. This encounter was not limited to a physical transaction. It was not a quick fix. When we come to Jesus with our need, Jesus offers us a comprehensive healing. At first, this woman seems to be looking only for a physical cure, but she receives spiritual restoration as well.

My initial experience of physical relief from back and tail-bone pain led me into deeper layers of healing for my soul. After that moment, I began to wonder whether other physical ailments I endured might have an emotional or spiritual root. In the past, I had assumed that the sinus infections I seemed to invite, host, and banish on a two-month rotation called for sleep and antibiotics. The redness around my eyes and nose called for prescription ointment. The tightness in my hips called for Advil and stretches.

It's not that these measures were bad. They were simply, and especially over the course of time, insufficient. They were my way of ignoring, denying, and rejecting the notion that my body was signaling a larger dis-ease, a deeper discord, within my spirit. I didn't want to address those deeper problems. I was afraid it would all amount to narcissistic attention on my every woe. I was also afraid of what that work of self-investigation might reveal.

I wonder if that bleeding woman started out like me—thinking that if she only found the right doctor or the proper herbal combination, if she only had a little more money, then she could fix her problem and return to her normal life. For me, beginning with that healing experience on the yoga mat and continuing through the years since, healing has meant looking not only at the surface level of pain in my body, but also at the deeper layers of hurt within my soul. In order for deeper healing to happen, I've needed to excavate dysfunctional patterns and false narratives I've told myself about my life. I've needed to slow down. I've needed to admit sin and neglect and denial. I've needed to acknowledge fears and anxieties. I've met with Anne and connected with a therapist and a spiritual director. I've become more honest with a group of trusted friends.

The nameless woman whose bleeding stopped was not only or even primarily cured of her pain. She was freed from her suffering. Healed. Saved. As a college student lying on a physical therapist's table, as a young mother sitting cross-legged on the floor, I too wanted more than relief from bodily illness and injury. I wanted healing.

Our bodies are always telling us something, always inviting us to reach out to God in the midst of our need so that we can receive whatever healing God has to offer. Healing doesn't always mean curing of disease or freedom from pain. I've experienced immediate relief from aches and illnesses, and I've endured chronic struggles that are unresolved to this day. I've witnessed healing in the midst of my mother-in-law's terminal cancer diagnosis, where the healing came by way of forgiveness and grief and laughter and acceptance of death. I've witnessed healing in our family as we accept the physical and cognitive limitations that come with disability and embrace the fullness of every person we encounter.

Healing will not look the same for everyone. It will not always involve bodily change. But it is available to all of us who know we need it. Like the nameless, destitute, desperate bleeding woman, we are all invited by Jesus to be made well.

CHAPTER 2

Jesus' Name Is Healer

At once Jesus realized that power had gone out from him.

—MARK 5:30

Ifeel self-conscious when I tell my story of sitting on a yoga mat in our upstairs hallway and feeling pain that had pressed upon me for months suddenly disappear. The memory seems overly simplistic and a little unbelievable. At the time, it felt like a miracle, a supernatural intervention from God. But it also seemed unimportant. Why would God care about my lower back pain? I'm attuned enough to the modern world to know that I could come up with other plausible explanations for what happened.

There's a neurobiological story for the change that took place in my body, and numerous fascinating books and TED talks and research journals explain how the brain and the body can connect to each other to bring a blissful cessation of pain. Simple, deliberate changes in how we breathe, for instance, can bring relief from pain and even change our physiology. According to journalist James Nestor, who wrote a book on the subject, learning how to breathe properly can even extend our life expectancy. Nestor also claims, from interviews with medical doctors, that breathing techniques can serve more effectively than medications as preventative maintenance against many of the ills of stressful modern life, including "irritable bowels, depression, an occasional tingling in the fingers."[1] On a similar note, in *The Body Keeps the Score*, a book about the physical impact of traumatic events, Dr. Bessel van der Kolk begins his section on treatment for trauma with breathing techniques. As many religious traditions have known for ages, something as simple as breathing can both prevent disease and bring healing.

Then there is the placebo effect, a mechanism that seems to trick the brain into thinking that an outside source of healing has intervened when really the brain itself has activated chemicals to do the healing work. Particular types of illnesses benefit the most from placebos, including my personal top two sources of chronic physical concern, gastrointestinal distress and back pain. Migraines, Parkinson's disease, and autoimmune disorders also all benefit from nonmedical intervention that prompts the brain to heal the body on its own. In *Suggestible You*, journalist Erik Vance explains that when encouraged to do so, the brain can self-medicate by producing endorphins, natural opioids that alleviate pain, as well as dopamine and serotonin that alleviate depression.[2]

Yet another science journalist, Melanie Warner, devotes a chapter of her book about alternative medicine to a man named Adam who overcame debilitating back pain without surgery or medication. His back scans, which remained constant, suggested that he should have been in pain, but somehow a combination of massage, deep breathing, and conversation left him pain-free. As Warner writes, when it comes to explanations for alleviation of pain, "we might need to look for answers in the mind and the brain as well as in the body."[3] When we are able to connect our bodies and our brains—whether through meditation or talk therapy or some other method—we may indeed experience relief from physical pain, and plenty of researchers these days can describe "miraculous" healings like mine in fairly simple biological terms. As Vance puts it, "Humans are deeply fallible creatures who build frameworks to explain the chaotic, confusing, and dangerous world they live in."[4]

In addition to all these books about the neurobiology of healing, there's no shortage of alternative medical treatments and religious practices that also offer ways to feel better. The burgeoning health and wellness industry—with vitamins and supplements and essential oils, mindfulness apps and seminars, and a steady stream of self-help titles—promises a happier, healthier me. I haven't personally experienced the efficacy of acupuncture, biofeedback, or group therapy, but I believe the reports that these methods have helped many. And of course, when it comes to alleviating pain and treating disease, a tremendous amount of relief has come to billions of people through conventional medication, whether anti-inflammatory drugs or pain relievers or antibiotics or chemotherapy treatments. But even with all these possibilities, millions of people who desperately want relief from pain nevertheless continue to suffer. It is not easy to delineate what we need in order to be made well.

In the course of trying to understand what happened to me on that yoga mat, I learned about foods that cause inflammation and emotional stress that leads to pain. I became fascinated

by the intricate explanations for how our bodies carry emotional suffering in physical ways, and by the corresponding
possibilities for healing that arise when we connect the body
to the mind and the emotions. I read Dr. Gabor Maté's book
When the Body Says No, which tells the flip side of the body's
capacity to heal itself. Maté offers story after story about men
and women whose unacknowledged psychological distress led
to significant pain and disease in their bodies. Stress harms
the hormonal, immune, and digestive systems of thousands of
patients, leading to chronic illness and even death.[5] I could
see the truth and relevance of his words as they related to my
emotionally repressed teenage self as well as to my struggles as
an adult. Maybe this "healing" wasn't spiritual at all. Maybe
it was just me waking up to the brilliance of my body's ability
to repair its own brokenness. Still, I kept coming back to Jesus.

Long before pop-neurobiology books explained this science
to people like me, Jesus was known as a healer. Depending on
how you count it, over 20 percent of the space in the gospel
records of Jesus' life depict Jesus as a healer.[6] We don't have
video records of Jesus' interactions with people, and even a
video of a paralyzed man starting to walk or a woman testi-
fying that her bleeding had stopped wouldn't convince all the
skeptics among us that they were healed through his presence.
But the women and men telling the stories about Jesus said he
was a healer. As pastor Bethany McKinney Fox writes, "[Jesus']
reputation as one who performed miraculous healings is about
as verifiable as we can get for an ancient figure."[7] Miraculous
healing was central to Jesus' identity and to his ministry.

Jesus' healing involved physical restoration for countless individuals, much as physicians set bones and prescribe
medications today. But as we see over and over again in
the Gospels, the personal, spiritual, and social healing that

Jesus offers goes further and wider than any bottle of pills or fiberglass cast ever could. I return to Jesus as a healer because I want to understand and experience healing that both takes my body seriously and goes deeper than my body. I want to participate in healing that extends beyond my own individual needs, as we see in the stories of Jesus not simply healing the sick but restoring them to community. For me to participate in a wider and broader work of healing, I need more than my annual physical or a list of steps for self-improvement. I need more than a lesson in breathing and brain chemistry, as fascinating and helpful as all those things are. I need help from outside myself. From the one whose very name means healing.

At the beginning of Matthew's gospel, Matthew tells his readers that Mary and Joseph will name their son Jesus. Then Matthew gives an explanation for Jesus' name: "For he will save his people from their sins" (Matthew 1:21 NRSV). To modern English readers, this explanation is not clear. How exactly is Jesus' name linked to his role as a savior? Here again, we encounter the Greek root *sozo* in the word *sosei*, which is translated "he will save" in our English Bibles. *Sosei* could also be translated "he will heal." This word connotes a comprehensive sense of whole-person redemption. But what does the word *sosei* have to do with the name Jesus? According to scholar James Edwards, "The word for *sozein* (another form of the root word *sozo*) in Hebrew and Aramaic is *yasha*, which is actually a variant of the Hebrew name of Jesus, Yeshua."[8] When Jesus was walking around on earth, no one actually called him Jesus. They called him Yeshua, Yasha. In Greek, Yasha becomes *sozein*. Tracing the breadcrumbs of these words suggests that Matthew sees Jesus' own name as a direct reference to God's redemptive, saving, healing power.

My friend Matt, a New Testament scholar, tells me that people in Jesus' day who met him on the street wouldn't have attached theological significance to his name. Hundreds of Jewish boys were named Yeshua, so to assume that the name automatically conjured thoughts of healing or salvation pushes the point too far.[9] That said, I think of the name Grace in our own day. When I meet a little girl named Grace, I don't always immediately think of God's compassionate and unmerited favor toward us. But the name nevertheless carries that meaning, and countless parents have given their child that name precisely because it reminds them of the unearned gift that comes to us in every human life. Similarly, while plenty of little boys were named Yeshua in Jesus' day, and their name might have held only a faint reminder that "the Lord saves/ heals," once Jesus actually began to heal people, I suspect his name took on greater significance. Looking back years later, we can say that Jesus' name is Savior. Jesus' name is Healer.[10]

As interesting and inspiring as I find this little etymological adventure, it still leaves me with the question of what it means that Jesus was a healer, both in name and in practice. Sources outside the Bible report that he was known as a miracle worker who healed people. With the possible exception of exorcisms, these aren't healings that can be explained through the placebo effect. Placebos cannot account for how the blind see, how the deaf hear, or how a shriveled hand becomes like new. Either they didn't happen the way the gospel writers tell us they did, or Jesus' miraculous healings are exactly that. Miraculous. Inexplicable. Surprising, welcome, supernatural interventions without clear biological explanation. Jesus brought something beyond the placebo effect to bear upon the hurting bodies, minds, and spirits of the people he encountered. That's why we—and they—call them miracles.

It would be easy and logical to assume that the whole point of Jesus' miracles is to prove his power and suggest his identity as the Son of God. As Jesus himself has the disciples report to John the Baptist, his healing demonstrates the generative, creative, and unusual power of God at work within him. His miracles announce the fact that the Messiah has come.

But Jesus also downplays his miraculous activity. There are times when he heals in secret and commands the recipients not to tell anyone else. When miracles do happen in public, he deflects attention from himself. And Jesus even hints that as much as this miraculous activity draws people to him, it also sometimes detracts from people's ability to understand God's deeper healing work in their lives. In the gospel of John, after Jesus feeds thousands of people with only a few loaves of bread, he mentions that the reason people are following him is because they "ate . . . and had [their] fill" (John 6:26), not because they believe in his message or his purpose. In fact, what seems to motivate Jesus over and over again when he performs miracles is not the performance part at all. What motivates him is compassion for people who are desperate to be made well. I'm not sure that Jesus was a big fan of miracles. I am convinced he was a big fan of helping people in need, and sometimes he used miracles to do so.

Jesus' miracles signal to his followers that he is the Messiah. They also demonstrate God's active love for people. But beyond these things, Jesus' miracles act as an invitation to a deeper, ongoing, transformative work of healing. In the dozens of longer accounts of Jesus' healings, healing extends beyond the moment of the miracle. Jesus' healings are marked by their intimacy, by his insistence on really seeing and listening to the people who need healing, by affirming and encouraging them, and by sending them forth with purpose into their community.

Jesus' very name is Healer, yet all this consideration of healing brings up the reality that for many people, then and now, pain remains and healing seems elusive. This conversation also brings up the question of disability and what to make of a child who is born with cerebral palsy or autism or an extra copy of the twenty-first chromosome in every cell of her body. I think back to one Easter morning when our daughter Penny was a toddler. A pair of men in our church asked if they could lay hands upon her and pray. We huddled in the corner of a bustling coffee hour, and my stomach constricted as I heard one of them say, "God, we pray you would heal this child of this evil Down syndrome."

I swallowed hard, muttered amen, and said thank you. Then I looked at our daughter, with the distinctive features of Down syndrome written into her body. Her eyes—intriguing and different with their resemblance to cut glass, holding an additional fold of skin. Her hands—small and soft and bearing an unusual line that spanned one side to the other of her palm. The flat bridge of her nose. The tiny ears. I looked at her and saw all the characteristics of a child with Down syndrome. I also saw someone who, as the psalmist wrote, had been fearfully and wonderfully made. Someone who had been created in love and for love. Someone who had been made well.

I didn't believe in the kind of healing this well-intentioned man of prayer wanted to offer Penny. I believed Jesus accepted and welcomed Penny and other people with disabilities as they were. I believed she had been created with a purpose, as she was. Yes, she bore brokenness within her body and soul, but not in any way that was more prominent or problematic than the ways I bore brokenness in my conventionally attractive face and normative body.

In his book *Wondrously Wounded*, theologian Brian Brock explores a Christian understanding of health and wholeness. He traces a history of early church fathers who saw children with disabilities as wonders created by God. Rather than seeing disability as a manifestation of the fallenness of creation, Brock argues that a Christian understanding of the human should both inform and subvert our understanding of disability and healing. Going back to Saint Augustine, for instance, Brock explains that Augustine thought sin was likely to cause us to reject and receive people using the wrong criteria. Because of our distorted understanding of human nature, we typically welcome and extol people who embody physical ideals instead of those who embody the virtue of love. According to Brock, Augustine saw it as an "injustice against God [to] claim that disabilities are nothing more than signs of the brokenness of creation."[11] Rather than seeing disability as a result of the fall, Augustine wondered in what way these infants and adults would display God's glory.

One of the problems of talking about Jesus' healing when it comes to disability arises from our misguided assumptions about who needs healing and what healing looks like. My friend Katherine, who survived a massive brain stem stroke and uses a wheelchair to this day, often encounters people who want to pray for her healing. Her husband Jay writes about Katherine's response: "She'll say, 'Of course you can pray for my physical healing—thank you so much—but can you also pray for my gossipy mouth or my negative spirit of judgment and comparison or for my marriage and kids?'"[12]

Similarly, Kyle Stevenson, a Baptist minister who has cerebral palsy, writes: "It's not uncommon that people who would see that I have a disability would ask me if I want them to pray. When I ask them, 'For what?', they would look dumbfounded and say, 'your healing.' When I would answer, 'From what?' They would not know what to say. They would look at my body and conclude it did not fit how they thought God designed bodies. They would decide something needed to be cured." He goes on to explore the idea that while he needs healing just as much as anyone else, that healing doesn't need to mean bodily change. Stevenson writes, "God does heal. However, God does not always cure, and there may not need to be a cure." He quotes scholar and Methodist minister Kathy Black: "Healing is finding 'a sense of well-being in a person's life, a sense of comfort, support, and peace.' Healing can happen amid having a disability."[13]

Jesus' emphasis in healing people with disabilities (and everyone else) is an emphasis on understanding ourselves as ones who already have been made well. Jesus' healing is not about curing disease or fixing disabled parts. He does not treat us as machines. Our bodies and souls have been marred by sin and pain and exclusion. Healing is about returning us to minds and bodies and spirits, in community, that have been made well.

And yet individuals still experience ongoing suffering in their given bodies. If Jesus' name was and is Healer, and if that healing is a comprehensive one that includes the body alongside a desire to eradicate pain and suffering, why does so much pain remain? A simplistic and wrong-headed answer locates the problem with the individual in pain. The pain of countless people has only been exacerbated by Christians who exhort them to have more faith, as if the amount of faith we possess can be handed to God in a cosmic exchange that returns healing to us. But Jesus heals people with the smallest shreds of faith. When his disciples are in a sinking boat, he first helps them and then tells them they have little faith (see Mark 4:35–41). More faith does not mean more healing.

Some people will live on this earth in pain, even with earnest prayer and fervent faith and active faithfulness. Duke professor Kate Bowler has written about her experience as a young woman with stage IV incurable cancer. She has endured dozens of surgeries and painful procedures. In the midst of it all, she also has experienced a profound sense of God's love and God's Spirit. She writes, "God's love was everywhere, sticking to everything. Love was in my husband's hand on my back, steadying me . . . love itself was suddenly more real to me than my own thoughts."[14] She has experienced a different level of connection and restoration to God than ever before. But she has not been cured. She has not been freed from pain.

In Paul's letter to the church in Rome, he writes about the "groaning" of creation (Romans 8:22). All God's creation—including our bodies and minds—has been subjected to frustration and groans. Paul links this groaning to hope. He offers a vision of a future in which the full and whole power of love is realized, a future in which all is made well. But that future is not yet here. Pain can bear witness to that which is not yet redeemed in this broken world of ours.

Healing is available to us now, and we can all open ourselves up to God's healing work. We can all participate in God's wider work of healing in the world around us. But we will also continue to groan in pain as we wait with hope for the fullness of God's love to be revealed and to make all things well.

Modern medicine has certainly—and blessedly—helped alleviate scores of instances of pain and suffering. We can give thanks to God that people with paralysis and epilepsy and debilitating skin conditions are not solely dependent on the hope of miraculous interventions. Yet even with all these advances, tens of millions of people experience chronic disease and chronic pain that not only takes a toll on their bodies but inhibits their ability to experience the fullness of community. Countless more experience an inner longing to be made well even if their bodies feel fine right now. Any honest account of healing has to admit and wrestle with this dissatisfying, uncomfortable, inscrutable mystery: While we affirm that God is always active in making us well, none of us will experience full healing. All of us will retain good longings that will go unmet. All of us will remain incomplete. And some of us will endure unspeakable pain and hardship along the way.

In the midst of modern experiences of pain and suffering, we need an integrated approach to healing just as much now as we did two thousand years ago. We need help from outside ourselves in order to receive that healing. The mysterious healing love of God is still available to us. God longs to bring our aching bodies, aching hearts, aching spirits, toward wholeness.

CHAPTER 3

Restored to Her Father

[Jesus] turned around in the crowd and asked, "Who touched
my clothes?"

"You see the people crowding against you," his disciples answered,
"and yet you can ask, 'Who touched me?'"

But Jesus kept looking around to see who had done it. Then the
woman, knowing what had happened to her, came and fell at his feet
and, trembling with fear, told him the whole truth. He said to her,
"Daughter . . ."

—MARK 5:30–34

In Jesus' day, as in ours, the easiest way to see the healing
power of God was through immediate physical transformation. For the bleeding woman, the bleeding stopped. For
me, my back felt all better. Countless other people can attest
to similar dramatic physical experiences of healing. Still, once
my back stopped hurting, the confusion and discord I felt

about my place in the world remained. Similarly, this woman's body stopped bleeding, but her poverty and social isolation remained. And of course, there are all the people—in the Gospels and in our world—who live every day with chronic physical pain and incurable disease and mental illness and everyday heartache, no matter how much they seek the restoration of body, mind, and spirit. Healing is not as simple as miraculous feel-better moments.

When individuals experience physical relief, we can celebrate with them, yet the biblical witness and our experiences all suggest there is more to healing than freedom from physical pain. As theologian John Swinton has written, our modern concept of health relies on the idea that we are healthy when we are free of illness or injury. Swinton suggests instead that we should turn to an ancient and biblical understanding of health. He writes, "Health is a relational concept which has nothing to do with our bodily shape, the number of our chromosomes or the sharpness of our minds. . . . The most hedonistic, intellectually astute athlete can be in need of healing (restoration to right relationship with God), and the most deeply impaired individuals can be healthy and indeed beautiful."[1]

Swinton also writes, "The Bible has no equivalent word to health as we might understand it within a contemporary biomedical context. The closest word is *shalom.*" He goes on to explain, "Shalom is not the absence of illness, disease, or disability. It has to do with the presence of God. . . . *Healing always has first and foremost to do with connecting and reconnecting people to God.*"[2]

In my own case, sitting on a yoga mat and experiencing relief from pain was only a beginning. That pain—and healing—drew my attention to the unrest within my soul. After that experience, every time my body manifested new concerns—strep throat, a headache, an aching wrist—I started to wonder whether I needed to pay attention to a deeper need. I asked God to help me bring prayer into my body. I wanted to learn how to connect my bodily experience to my emotions and memories, to whatever the Spirit might be inviting me to understand.

For example, one Labor Day we were driving home from the beach after a delightful summer vacation. The next day heralded the start of the school year, with all its demands—the rush of packing lunches and wiping counters and taking out the recycling and keeping up with the laundry, the hours of driving our children to various afternoon activities, the school concerts and PTO meetings and church council meetings and social obligations in the evening. On that car ride home, I sneezed uncontrollably for over an hour.

I mused out loud about what was happening all of a sudden in my body, and from the back seat William chimed in, "I think you're allergic to change."

He named the deeper truth. That just as some of us have bodies that fight dust motes with a dramatic flow of mucous to purge those invaders from the sinuses, so too my body was mounting an unwitting defense against the change of pace that starting school represented. My body was showing me my fear of the upcoming weeks, fear I hadn't been aware of. But once William named it for me, I knew how to pray. And every time I felt that tingle in my nostrils, I paused and closed my eyes and reminded myself of the truth: *I am safe. There is nothing to fear. The Lord is with me.*

On the surface, Jesus offers physical repair for individuals when he heals them. But story after story in the Gospels reveals a deeper and broader understanding of what it means to be made well. In Luke 5, when a group of friends bring a paralyzed man to Jesus, Jesus first tells him his sins are forgiven. Only later does Jesus restore mobility to the man's legs. Jesus prompts everyone present, and us as readers thousands of years later, to wonder whether receiving forgiveness is akin to being able to walk again. If anything, in this scene, walking again seems peripheral to the main event—the proclamation that this man's sins are forgiven. His newfound ability to walk testifies to the deeper spiritual healing that comes through forgiveness.

And just as Jesus tells this woman who has been bleeding "Your faith has *healed* you," so Jesus uses the exact same words when addressing a "sinful" woman who has poured perfume on his feet. Most English Bibles translate this interaction with Jesus saying "Your faith has *saved* you," but in Greek there is no distinction between what Jesus says to the bleeding woman and the woman who has received forgiveness. Elsewhere, when Jesus has dinner with the tax collector Zacchaeus who then gives half his money to the poor, Jesus proclaims that "today salvation has come to this house" (Luke 19:9). In Greek that word, salvation, is *soteria*. Again, it comes from that same root, *sozo*. Salvation has come to this house. Healing has come to this house. Deliverance has come to this house today.

In all these cases, Jesus uses interchangeable language to offer spiritual freedom and physical transformation. With the bleeding woman, this same comprehensive approach to healing becomes evident. Here, we first see how Jesus' power restores her to physical well-being. Later, we will see how it restores her to her broader community. But this encounter also demonstrates that for Jesus, another fundamental aspect of healing is restoring us to God.

After she reaches out to Jesus, this nameless woman almost slips away in the crowd. Her body has stopped bleeding. She has been healed, and she hopes to remain unnoticed. But Jesus calls her out. Mark makes it clear that she isn't coming before Jesus with a sense of accomplishment or even, primarily, gratitude. Rather, she comes trembling with fear.

Even today, constant menstrual bleeding would be smelly and messy and potentially shameful. In Jesus' day, in a time without sanitary products and flushing toilets, in a time without showers and washing machines, we can hardly conceive what this woman's life would have been like. She lived in a culture where women were already considered inferior to men, and her condition meant she could not bear children. In a social context that equated childbearing with personal worth, she was cut off from herself as a woman, cut off from honor, cut off from giving birth to future generations.[3]

Her reluctance to approach Jesus suggests that she comes forward expecting rebuke, perhaps even punishment, for her brazen presence and subversive action. She is an unclean woman who has just touched a holy man without permission. She has every reason to fear.

But Jesus offers no rebuke. Instead, Jesus listens while she tells her story. We can almost feel the disciples checking their watches, trying to catch his eye, tilting their heads in the direction of Jairus's house. From their perspective, she is not supposed to divert Jesus' attention. She is not worthy of all this time. But even as they tap their feet, we can also imagine Jesus' gaze softening. Mark doesn't give details about Jesus' posture here, but in so many other personal encounters, the gospel writers tell us explicitly that while Jesus listens to people, he feels love, compassion, and even grief at the pain they have experienced.[4] We don't get her words directly, though we can imagine from Mark's earlier list of details what she tells Jesus about herself. She offers a story of years of rejection, disappointment, and pain. A story in which things only got worse. A story that became so close to hopeless that she was willing to take the risk of entering this crowd and reaching out.

And then comes the word she might not have known she was waiting for. Jesus gives her a name. He calls her *Daughter*. He gently and graciously and publicly acknowledges her humanity in the most tender and intimate terms. For Jesus, healing is not simply a matter of physical transformation. Healing is about underscoring the deep affection, ongoing care, and everlasting love that God has for each one of us.

In order to feel the full impact of Jesus' name for this woman, we need to move backward in the narrative. Mark sets his readers up for this moment. Scholars call this passage an example of a "Markan sandwich," where one story—the story of Jairus—is interrupted with another story, the story of the bleeding woman. Mark doesn't employ this strategy simply to report events in the order they transpired. He could have easily finished Jairus's story and then told the reader what had happened on the way to Jairus's house. No, Mark places these stories this way—with Jairus as the "bread" and the woman's healing as the "meat"—to prompt the reader to compare and contrast them.

The contrast becomes clear immediately. Jairus is a man with a name, with money, with religious and cultural power, and with a family. This woman is unnamed, poor, unclean, in pain, and alone. The two figures begin as direct opposites. But a closer look reveals what links them together. Jairus has approached Jesus on behalf of his twelve-year-old daughter. Mark also tells us the woman has been bleeding for twelve years. This repeated number becomes the first clue that the two stories might connect.

Then Jesus names the woman *Daughter*. Our attention here should flicker back to that same word used just a few sentences earlier. Jairus has humbled himself before Jesus and begged for Jesus' help on behalf of his beloved child. And here Jesus publicly calls this outcast woman by the same intimate name. We are invited to think that Jesus' love for this woman—God's love for this woman—is as fierce and protective and unyielding as Jairus's love for his little girl.

This moment stands out for its intimacy, yet it is also in keeping with the way Jesus insists that his followers relate to God. In contrast to the way God is usually named throughout the Jewish Scriptures, Jesus calls God *Father*. Exclusively. The only way Jesus prays is by calling God Father. And perhaps that's to be expected. Jesus is known as the Son of God, so it might seem natural for him to call God by the name Father. We might even assume this term is reserved for Jesus' use, a way for him to set himself apart when referencing God.

But Jesus insists that his disciples do the same. "Teach us to pray," they say. He doesn't begin with the customary Jewish address to God as king and creator of the universe. Instead, he instructs them to pray, "Our Father."[5] Elsewhere, Jesus compares God to a father giving bread to his children when they ask. He describes God as a father running to greet his wayward son with great joy when that son returns home. Jesus even calls his disciples "little ones," as if to emphasize their status as children, children of God.[6] As theologian Janet Martin Soskice points out, "God is described as 'father' more than 170 times in the New Testament, and is never invoked in prayer by any other title. God is designated 'father' only eleven times in the entire Old Testament, and is never invoked as such in prayer."[7] In other words, Jesus unexpectedly invites the bleeding woman, alongside all his other followers, to know God primarily as a good and loving Father and to know themselves primarily as God's children.

Over and over and over again, Jesus says, "God is your father." He is not portraying God as a father in order to double down on God as a figure of masculine might. Soskice explains, the God of the Bible is the same God who labors like a birthing woman in the book of Isaiah, the same God who in the New Testament gives birth, like a mother, to each person who claims faith in Jesus. The reason Jesus insists on calling God Father is to invite us into an intimate relationship with God. A relationship that is personal, permanent, and transformative. A relationship that establishes God's love and responsibility as a parent. A relationship that conveys our identity as beloved children who can come to God and ask for help.

In invoking this term, Jesus is not trying to assert patriarchy or take away God's other roles—king, judge, Lord, creator. He is simply claiming that the primary way we are to relate to God is as children of a loving father. I began to understand this idea when our kids were little and their dad became a head of school. Overnight, Peter was invested with new power. He now held the responsibility to oversee all the operations of the school, to hire and fire faculty, and to decide whether and when students should be expelled. We quickly learned that this new status changed how other people saw him. Some asked him for favors standing in line at the hardware store. Others didn't invite us to parties, because they were worried about what he might think of their behavior. To most people in our town, Peter is known only in his role at the school.

But at the end of the day, when Peter walks through the playroom door, our kids look up from whatever they're doing and they see their dad. They see the guy who will teach them how to hold a handstand and share their excitement over the latest

Star Wars movie. The one they might complain to when their sibling gets extra dessert. The one who reads books to them and cheers for the Yankees with them and wrestles with them and tucks them into bed. They know he is the head of school. They even have a sense of the weighty responsibilities that accompany his job. But they have never approached him as someone who might kick them out. Our kids approach Peter as their father. They approach him as the one who does "silly hands" at the dinner table and who plays ping-pong with them and who also corrects them for chewing with their mouths open and chastises them when they sneak screen time.

Jesus invites everyone who follows him to know God as Father and to know themselves as children, as sons and daughters in intimate, dependent relationships with God. He even goes so far as to say, "Unless you change and become like little children, you will never enter the kingdom of heaven" (Matthew 18:3). When Jesus names this woman *Daughter*, he essentially welcomes her into his family. He doesn't simply accept her or affirm her. He goes beyond that to underscore her belovedness as one created and welcomed by God. Part of the healing offered to all of us is to understand our belovedness.

Catholic priest and scholar Henri Nouwen experienced this sense of belovedness when he decided to move from a prestigious teaching position at Yale Divinity School to L'Arche—a community where neurotypical people and people with intellectual disabilities live side by side. There, Nouwen interacted with men and women who were not impressed by his credentials but simply cared for him. They loved him as he was rather than for what he could do for them. For Nouwen, healing came through an understanding of himself as the beloved of God.[8]

Pastor and author Osheta Moore also writes about belovedness as the foundation for the healing work of antiracist peacemaking. "Belovedness . . . undoes our striving and proving," she writes. "The only thing you should be focused on is owning your Belovedness, proclaiming my Belovedness, and working to become the Beloved Community."[9] When the bleeding woman becomes *Daughter*, she becomes one who can own her belovedness, proclaim the belovedness of those around her, and work to bring belovedness into her community.

Over these past six years, I have received healing in many ways, but even after all this time, I struggle to believe that my value comes from God's love and not my performance or perfection. I still long for approval and commendation from other people. I still have too many nights when a glass of wine—or two or three—feels like a better solution to my anxieties than a few minutes of prayer or curling up with a good book. Various parts of my body still flare up with pain that seems more related to stress than to any particular physical illness or injury.

For all these years, I have cycled through believing that I am God's beloved and then falling back into old patterns of shame and anxiety. By the time the winter of 2020 rolled around, I had become tired of what felt like a constant need for more inner work, greater self-reflection, more inner healing. I wondered when "self-care" became self-indulgence, whether healing was truly possible, and whether I had the energy for it. I met by video with Anne in the midst of this weariness, and I told her I wanted to be done. I had worked hard to address painful memories. I had learned new ways to pray and meditate. I wanted to make a deal with God that we had taken this healing experience far enough. In that conversation, I also told Anne the story of the bleeding woman and how Jesus just keeps going with her healing—first the physical, and then naming her *Daughter*, and then sending her forth with a blessing. I talked about how I both longed for that comprehensive healing and felt tired by the thought of it. Anne smiled and nodded and said, "Well, the only way healing happens is if the love goes deeper than the wound."

The only way healing happens is if the love goes deeper than the wound.

Jesus isn't inviting me to more healing because he wants me to work harder. He doesn't call the bleeding woman out in order to shame her or take credit or offer advice. He invites each one of us to more healing because he wants us to know his love more deeply. No matter how long it takes, he wants the love to go deeper than the wounds.

When I think of God as our Father, I think of us as toddlers learning to walk. Imagine a little one who takes two tottering steps and then falls over. How does a loving mom or dad respond? Her mother doesn't chastise her for being unsteady on her feet. She doesn't scowl at the failed effort. She whoops with delight. Her father helps her off the ground. They take a video to commemorate the moment and celebrate.

I lost that sense of radical acceptance and unconditional love somewhere along the way. I graduated from high school with the dubious distinction of being named in the yearbook as the person with the longest "brag sheet." Apparently, my list of activities, leadership positions, awards, and commendations stretched longer than anyone else's. I stood as an extreme example of someone desperately hoping to find acceptance by way of achievement. But as my multiple hospital stays in high school and college attest, achieving more and more did not provide the sense of personal approval I craved. Even once I had recovered from my stomach paralysis and started my first job out of college, I worked so hard and long that every few months I ended up in bed for ten days with some sort of respiratory infection. I was twenty-three years old, and four or five times a year I couldn't function, because I had worked myself into illness.

I needed to change my behavior—to learn how to relax, make space for exercise, turn off the computer at a reasonable hour. But underneath that behavior, I needed to learn that I had a Father who loved me, not for my performance or achievement, but rather because he had created me with delight and with good purposes in mind. I called God *Father* every week at church and in my own prayer time, but I didn't live with the certainty of that grounding love. I still tried to earn it. Day after day after day. That relentless striving literally made me sick.

Then, after Penny was born, I experienced my own deep delight in our child, not for anything she accomplished but simply in the fact of her life, in the gift of her presence. I suspect that becoming a parent would have taught me something about God's unconditional love under any circumstances, but because Penny also was born with a diagnosis of Down syndrome, she helped me understand love even more. I knew that Penny would not grow up with the same accolades that I received. She would not be valued by our society for her grades or athletic achievements or high earning potential. Yet every day brought a reminder of her belovedness. Her soft skin, her sparkling eyes, her sweet expressions of care and encouragement for other people, her perseverance, her love for reading—I loved her for all the things that made her who she was. I didn't need to work to love her. And there was nothing she could ever do to make me love her less. It is this type of love that Jesus wants us to receive when he insists we call God Father. As I experienced love for Penny, I began to understand that every human life is endowed with inestimable worth. Even mine.

Most of us have not inherited a sense of ourselves as the beloved of God, nor a sense of ourselves as the image bearers of love. Even among those of us who follow Jesus, we easily determine who we are by the good things we do. We measure ourselves by how well we have loved other people or how faithfully we have attended church or volunteered at a local soup kitchen. In this mindset, just as in our culture, what I do tells me who I am. Achievement—whether for Jesus or for my employer—equals identity.

But Jesus says that we are beloved before we do anything right, and after we've done everything wrong.

Jesus says that our belovedness comes first. Belovedness is our identity, and it is not an identity we achieve. What we do does not determine who we are.

Healing is not an achievement. Rather, it is an invitation to more fully experience God's love for us. As I recognized my own deep need to receive God's healing as a gift from a loving Father to a beloved daughter, I heeded the advice of a series of spiritual teachers who recommended contemplative prayer as a way to experience God's love. Every day I set a timer, usually for five or ten minutes, depending on how impatient I was feeling. And then I sat—eyes closed, cross-legged, breathing slowly and deeply. I tried to keep my to-do list and anxieties at bay and to breathe in and out the words: *God is love.* Or, *I am loved.* Or, *Love is patient.* Or, *I have a loving Father.*[10] I wanted to receive the sense of peace and belonging and wholeness that would come from resting in God's presence. I did this day after day for many months. It was peaceful, but I wouldn't have called it transformative, until one day I had what I think I can call a vision. I saw myself walking toward God, and being invited to climb up into God's lap like a little child. Before I accepted the invitation, I decided to bring God a few things. I brought my diplomas from college and seminary. I brought awards I've won. I brought our three children, proof of my devotion and hard work for our family. I brought the books I've written. When I was done presenting God with my accomplishments, I was ready to climb up.

I won't say I heard an audible voice, but I had a very clear sense of what God wanted me to understand at that moment. *There's no room for you on top of all these achievements.*

I looked at the pile. So many objects, with such sharp edges, stacked so precariously.

If you want to know my love, you'll have to take them away.

And so I went through the process in reverse. I removed the framed words demonstrating my degrees, the bronze statues indicating awards, the pile of books. I took them away until God's lap was empty and I could find a place to rest. To receive God's embrace. To be the beloved. And to repeat that process daily, if needed, as an ongoing reminder that the love of God comes first, for who I am, not what I do. God offered me a way to see that my accomplishments and awards are not beloved. I am God's beloved. We are God's beloved.

I told that story to a friend of mine, and she laughed. "It would never cross my mind to bring God my accomplishments," she said. "But I can see myself never getting onto his lap, because I insisted that other people go ahead of me. I'm the person who would miss out on that invitation because I never believed the invitation was really for me."

We are all like bumbling children taking wobbly steps forward and falling over. We are all struggling to believe that amid our frailty and sin, we approach a God who rejoices in us. We are all like the nameless, bleeding woman, trying so hard, working so tirelessly to fix ourselves, to not be a bother, believing the lies that we have told ourselves and have heard from our culture—that we are unlovable, that we don't deserve God's kindness, that we should stay small and quiet and sneak up behind Jesus in the crowd just in case this miracle worker, this last-ditch effort, might heal us. Perhaps, like this woman, we are fearful and ashamed and defensive even after we've experienced some healing, and we try to explain what happened. And then, Jesus calls us *Daughter. Son. Beloved.* And when we begin to live in that love, when our actions flow from that love, when our behavior is transformed by that love, we receive healing. We are restored to ourselves and to God. We experience that personal integration of mind and body and spirit. We, the ones who are called and known as beloved, are then called and equipped to pour that same love out into the world.

CHAPTER 4

Restored to Community

[Jesus] turned around in the crowd and asked, "Who touched my clothes?"

"You see the people crowding against you," his disciples answered, "and yet you can ask, 'Who touched me?'"

But Jesus kept looking around to see who had done it. Then the woman, knowing what had happened to her, came and fell at his feet and, trembling with fear, told him the whole truth.

—MARK 5:30–33

One morning in the winter of 2003, the phone rang while I was still in bed. My mother-in-law, whom we now call Grand Penny, asked to talk to Peter. She told him she had been diagnosed with liver cancer. She said the tumor was the size of a grapefruit.

Grand Penny had lived alone for years. She and Peter's dad divorced when he was six, and she never remarried.

For most of Peter's life, his mom struggled with depression. She took multiple medications with various undesirable side effects. She saw a therapist twice a week and attended weekly group therapy sessions to try to work through years of loneliness and pain and trauma that went back to her own childhood. And now she was facing a serious, potentially terminal, diagnosis.

We flew to New Orleans to be with her the next day. By then, word of her illness had spread, and the following morning, local family members and friends convened in her home. It wasn't an organized effort. But somehow everyone knew that the way to care for her, the way to care for ourselves in the face of this distressing news, was to arrive at her doorstep and organize her house.

Friends from childhood, friends from the neighborhood, people from church, her sisters, Peter and I—we worked all day. We scrubbed mildew off the ceilings and mold off the deck. We rearranged furniture and threw away broken blinds and chipped pots and dried-up pens and markers. That evening, someone took the flowers that had been arriving in a steady stream and redistributed them among ten vases of colored glass along her mantle. It was a day of blessing.

Grand Penny died six months later. And yet that day stands in my memory as the beginning of her healing. For years, she had been curled up into isolation and self-recrimination and shame. But that day, she received a message of love from her community, and it changed her. Even as she went on to endure a major surgery and the burning pain of radiation and the fatigue of recovery, even as the cancer markers in her blood began to rise, she was healing. She reached out to her siblings and her parents for reconciliation. She returned to church and asked for help to know where she would be going once she died. She gave thanks. She forgave, and she asked for forgiveness.

What's more, she did not walk through her illness alone. She was accompanied every step of the way by people who loved her. People from church, from childhood, from high school and college and her years in Manhattan stopped by or flew down to visit. Her sisters, her children, and multiple friends accompanied her through each day of treatment. On the day she died, both of her sons were by her side. Family and friends filled the room. She experienced the healing love of God through the healing love of the people around her.

When I encounter the bleeding woman in Mark's gospel, I think of Peter's mom. Grand Penny needed to be restored to God as much as—perhaps more than—she needed any physical act of healing. She needed to know that Jesus called her *Daughter*. And Grand Penny, like the bleeding woman, also needed to be restored to her community. As illness consumed her body, she experienced saving, restorative, healing love. And the community who received her was a crucial component of that healing.

Of all four canonical gospels,[1] Mark's offers the shortest account of Jesus' ministry. He often jumps from one scene to the next with the words *immediately* or *suddenly*. But Mark lingers with this woman. Maybe that's because Jesus himself lingered with her. Even after her bleeding has stopped, Jesus insists on calling her forward. Everything slows down. The disciples nudge each other with impatience. Jairus feels panic rising in his chest as Jesus seems to have forgotten about his little girl. Presumably the large crowd that has been swept up in the walk to Jairus's house also pauses, wondering why Jesus suddenly stands still. After he hears the woman's story, Jesus makes sure that everyone nearby knows what has happened. He announces publicly that she has been made well.

Jesus doesn't always draw this type of attention to people who have received his healing touch. Just a few verses later, when Jesus heals Jairus's daughter, he issues "strict orders not to let anyone know about this" (5:43). Later, in Mark 7, Jesus takes a man who is deaf and mute "away from the crowd" (v. 33). Only then does Jesus heal him, with instructions not to tell anyone what has happened. And in Mark 8, Jesus heals a blind man and tells him not to go into the village. Scholars call this pattern in Mark the "messianic secret," whereby Jesus hides his identity as the anointed one sent by God, an identity that could be confirmed by the power to miraculously heal. In contrast, here Jesus makes sure that everyone around this woman knows what has happened.

When the woman finally presents herself to Jesus, Mark tells us she is trembling with fear. Her bleeding has stopped, but all of a sudden she is afraid that she has been thrust back into her old story of social shame and rejection. The one who has begun to knit her back together now stands in a position to condemn her, to tear her apart. In front of everyone.

But Jesus does not condemn her. Instead he extols her for her faith and names her *Daughter*. And in so doing, Jesus makes it clear to everyone nearby—his disciples, the crowd, even the synagogue leader—that this woman should be fully restored and welcomed into their social, religious, economic, and communal life. As we have already explored, her healing is not simply a matter of physical cure. It involves her whole self. And here we see this healing extend beyond this woman's restoration to self, beyond her restoration to God. Her healing is also a restoration to community. For Jesus, healing is never reduced to an individual who suddenly feels better. For Jesus, healing is always more.

Story after story echoes Jesus' concern here that individuals be restored to community. In the very beginning of Mark's gospel, Jesus heals a man with leprosy and instructs him to present himself to the temple priests. This action allows him to return to communal worship, to reenter society (Mark 1:40–44). When Jesus sees a funeral procession in which a widow is grieving the loss of her only son, not only does Jesus resuscitate the son, but, Luke writes, "[Jesus gives] him back to his mother" (7:15). The healing is for the son, and for his mother. It is also for all the mourners present who have had their grief turned to joy (Luke 7:11–17). Or in another story, when Bartimaeus receives his sight, not only is he now able to see, but he also goes on to join Jesus' followers (Mark 10:46–52). After Jesus exorcises the demons from a man living among the tombs, he sends the man back to his people (Mark 5:1–20). In each of these cases, Jesus shifts attention away from his own power to heal, and he insists that the individuals who have received healing be reconnected to other people. Healing involves restoration to self, to God, and to the wider community.

Theoretically, we now erect fewer barriers to community for those experiencing illness and disability than in Jesus' day. We have wheelchairs and modern medicine and Individualized Education Plans. But illness and disability still bring with them isolation because of social stigma and the limitations of our built environments. Our society still tells a story about the shame and relative lack of value for human beings not living in "ideal" bodies. People with chronic illness, pain, and disability still testify to the isolation and rejection they experience in many communal settings.

In *Disability and the Way of Jesus*, Bethany McKinney Fox includes the story of Jean, a woman whose back was bent forward because of scoliosis and a previous surgery. Jean writes of various ways she was excluded by the church and by her community. One friend told Jean that she was embarrassed to be seen with her in public.[2] Parents of children with developmental disabilities who make unexpected noises in church often relate how their family has been asked to leave the sanctuary if they cannot keep their child quiet. My friend Jessica, who walks with canes for support because of cerebral palsy, talks about how she researches the public transportation system of any city she hopes to visit because she knows that some cities have been built to welcome her, while others seem built to exclude.

Countless other people experience isolation and shame and disconnection from community, even without overt illness or disability. The recent COVID-19 pandemic meant that hundreds of millions of people began to live in greater isolation from their neighbors, friends, coworkers, and even family members. And we felt that isolation—in our bodies, minds, and spirits. Even before the pandemic, scholars had begun to take note of an epidemic of loneliness. According to a report from the Centers for Disease Control, "Social isolation significantly increased a person's risk of premature death from all causes, a risk that may rival those of smoking, obesity, and physical inactivity." Their report explains that loneliness is associated with increased risks of dementia, heart disease, stroke, depression, and anxiety, as well as a higher likelihood of death from these conditions, including death by suicide.[3] Social isolation, they say, has the same negative health effects as smoking fifteen cigarettes a day. The United Kingdom has even appointed a "minister of loneliness" within its cabinet to try to address the problem. When humans live in isolation from one another, we suffer. Conversely, when humans connect in meaningful ways to one another, we heal.

As Dr. Bessel van der Kolk, author of *The Body Keeps the Score*, writes, "Traumatized human beings recover in the context of relationships." He mentions families, religious communities, and Alcoholics Anonymous meetings as places where this type of recovery can happen.[4] Although scientists have developed some medications that alleviate the symptoms of addictive behavior, millions of people struggling with addiction testify to the simple power of gathering in community and sharing their stories of pain and relapse and triumph and being accepted as they are. Researchers have backed up the anecdotal data that champions the twelve-step program's support model. According to the Stanford Medicine News Center, a review of thirty-five studies with over ten thousand participants concluded, "AA was nearly always found to be more effective than psychotherapy in achieving abstinence. In addition, most studies showed that AA participation lowered health care costs."[5] A report in the *Journal of Alcohol Studies* determined that "recovering alcoholics who help other alcoholics maintain long-term sobriety following formal treatment are themselves better able to maintain their own sobriety."[6] In other words, relationships and social connection seem to be the most important factors in recovery from alcohol use disorder.

I saw the healing power of community firsthand last summer when our girls and I volunteered at Hope Heals Camp. This camp was founded by Jay and Katherine Wolf. As I mentioned earlier, Katherine lived through a massive brain stem stroke at the age of twenty-six, and while she credits the surgeons and therapists and medications that helped her recover, both she and Jay also look to the community of people who gathered around them to help out with practical needs, pray and pray some more, and provide the care of laughter and tears and emotional support. Jay and Katherine have now founded a camp for families who are affected in some way by disability. We met one family who had come as volunteers, even though they had attended the camp as campers in previous years. Their son lost his feet in a traumatic accident, and for a few years the whole family had come to Hope Heals to receive care from a community of people who accepted, supported, and loved them all as they were. But now, a few years after the accident, this family decided to return to camp as volunteers rather than as campers. Nothing had changed about their son's body, but he and his parents were ready to offer care to others. This family continues to need—and seek out—healing, even as they also are ready to participate in offering that same care to others in positions of need.

We often think about healing in individualistic terms, but even our language reflects its communal nature. *Hospital* and *hospitality* share the same root. To welcome people into our homes and into our lives is an act of healing. *Salve* and *salvation* share the same root. To care physically for another human is related to rescuing that person from spiritual harm.

Dr. Victoria Sweet served for years as a physician at Laguna Honda, an "almshouse"—a hospital for people who cannot take care of themselves and have no means to pay for services. In her memoir about this experience, she describes the origins of hospitals: "They were specifically Western and Christian institutions, not Greek or Roman. . . . It was the Christian monastery of the Middle Ages that originated the hospital system we know today."[7] She goes on to detail the care that comes to patients through "inefficient" practices of doctors and nurses simply sitting with them in silence, the healing that comes to some patients not through their medication but through their newfound community. Again, many people with disabilities testify to the fact that their "suffering" is far more a social experience than it is a physical one. Even in the twenty-first century, healing comes by way of community.

Jesus' insistence on returning the bleeding woman to her community helps us see that healing takes place within a wider social context. In publicly commending this woman and proclaiming her made well, Jesus does everything he can to ensure she will be welcomed by those around her. Healing does not only come from miraculous physical transformation. It does not only come from reconnecting mind, body, and spirit. Nor does it arise only out of experiencing forgiveness or acceptance by God. Healing also happens when we are received as a vital member of a community, in love. Healing happens when we know we are welcomed, when we know we belong.

Jesus' ministry of healing weds the personal and social aspects of healing in a way that most of our churches and our secular culture haven't managed to do. For him, the fragmented self is fully restored only in and as it is restored to community, and the community is made whole only in and as the individual members experience shalom. The presence of God—creator, image-maker, abounding in love and forgiveness—is known and experienced not only as we connect body, mind, and spirit, but also as we connect one to another.

Healing depends upon God. And healing depends upon us. Restored to ourselves. Restored to God. And restored to one another. We need Jesus, and we need each other, to be made well.

CHAPTER 5

Healing for All

While Jesus was still speaking, some people came from the house of Jairus, the synagogue leader. "Your daughter is dead," they said. "Why bother the teacher anymore?"

—MARK 5:35

I hated Flannery O'Connor's short stories the first time I read them, as a sophomore in high school English class. For anyone who hasn't encountered this quixotic southern writer, she portrays humanity in the fullness of what John Calvin called our "total depravity." In O'Connor's fiction, everyone is a sinner in need of grace, especially the people who are least likely to understand themselves that way. Many of her stories end with a socially respectable, "nice" Christian person facing a gory death.

Even though they left me rattled, those stories stuck with me. I returned to them in college and then again as a seminary student. The one that first turned my mind from hatred to appreciation was "Revelation." It portrays a southern white woman, Ruby Turpin, who feels eternally grateful that Jesus did not make her like other people, especially like Black people (she uses a pejorative slur here) and what she calls "white trash."

In the midst of her internal reverie about her own fabulous place in society, an ugly white girl named Mary Grace hurls a textbook at Mrs. Turpin and says, "Go back to hell where you came from, you old warthog." Ruby Turpin is shocked by these impudent words and this violent assault, yet she also recognizes that Mary Grace has been the conduit of a message from God. Mrs. Turpin abhors this message. She doesn't understand it. But she also recognizes that these words are from Jesus for her.

The story ends with Mrs. Turpin arguing with God: "What do you send me a message like that for? . . . Why me? It's no trash around here, black or white, that I haven't given to. And break my back to the bone every day working. And do for the church. . . . How am I a hog? Exactly how am I like them?" After she shouts at God, she receives a vision of a line of people dancing their way into heaven. At the front of the line are the people Mrs. Turpin is most likely to think don't deserve to be there, or at least the ones who she thinks deserve to take their spots in the back: Black people, poor white people who do not behave respectably, "freaks and lunatics," everyone she has judged in her heart throughout the previous pages. "And bringing up the end of the procession was a tribe of people whom she recognized at once as those who, like herself, had always had a little of everything and the God-given wit to use it right."[1] The story ends with an open question for Ruby Turpin: Will she take her place at the back of the line? Will she join this chorus of uncomfortably human worshipers? Or will she die in isolation? Will she go to hell in order to keep her respectability?

In much of her fiction, O'Connor prompts "nice" white people to wonder about their position before God. She uses race, class, illness, and disability to force readers to reckon with the uncomfortable claim that these social outcasts are also the ones most likely to receive God's grace. I didn't fully understand what O'Connor was doing in her stories when I first read them, and I suspect some of my ignorance came because they were written to confront people like me. O'Connor constantly asks, Can people like me understand our need for grace? Can we admit our need for healing?

It wouldn't be surprising to find a desperate, bleeding woman in the pages of Flannery O'Connor's stories, and it wouldn't be surprising for that woman to be the clear recipient of God's grace. And if a woman like this did show up in O'Connor's pages, we would start looking for her nice, respectable counterpart, the able-bodied, religiously observant, responsible citizen who judges the bleeding woman for her illness and feels self-satisfied by their own good health. In Mark 5, we find this same type of contrast between a marginalized woman and a powerful man at the center of society. And just as O'Connor's stories prompt uncomfortable questions about God's posture toward respectable people, Mark might want us to wonder about Jairus's position before Jesus.

Mark mentions three times that Jairus—this powerful man who stands in contrast to the nameless woman—is a local synagogue leader. Three times. Synagogue leader. Synagogue leader. Synagogue leader. I learned in seminary that repetition in the Bible means *pay close attention*. When the Bible was written, most people were illiterate. They would hear the text read aloud rather than read it on their own, so repeated words would stand out. In addition, early copies of the Bible did not include punctuation. There were no exclamation points

or italicized words. All this is to say, when Mark keeps not-
ing Jairus's name and his title, it is as if he has underlined,
highlighted, and circled this indication of Jairus's status in
his community.

At first, this emphasis might seem like a way to demonstrate Jesus' rising importance in Galilee. Jesus is becoming
powerful enough that even the leaders seek him out. But Jesus'
encounters with synagogue leaders generally do not go well.
Earlier in Mark, Jesus heals a man in the synagogue on the
Sabbath. There ensues a dramatic and emotional interaction
between Jesus and the religious leaders. The religious leaders
interpret Jesus' action as a violation of laws against "working" on the Sabbath. Jesus insists that acts of compassion are
always compatible with God's law. As scholar Timothy Gombis writes, for Jesus, "there is a generosity of spirit that main-
tains that it is always appropriate to restore, to give life, and to
heal."[2] But for the religious leaders, there is more than Sabbath
law at stake here. Jesus seems to be subverting their religious
authority and power when he heals on the Sabbath and in the
synagogue. After one such incident, Mark writes, "then the
Pharisees went out and began to plot with the Herodians how
they might kill Jesus" (Mark 3:6). Jesus' confrontation with
leaders in the synagogue leads to death threats.

Then, immediately after this scene with Jairus, Jesus shows
up in a synagogue in a different town where again, people
"took offense at him" (Mark 6:3). Similarly, in Luke, Jesus
provokes dramatic and negative reactions in the synagogue.
Luke describes the leaders as so "furious" at one point that
they attempt to throw Jesus off a cliff (4:28–30). Later, Jesus
yet again heals someone in the synagogue and engages in a
heated dispute with the leaders, who, Luke reports, "were
humiliated" (13:10–17).[3] Jesus, it seems, is no friend to

synagogue leaders. And healing is often at the center of the contention between them.

So when Mark draws attention to Jairus's position, is he signaling Jesus' status or alerting the reader to potential conflict? Or is he simply emphasizing the dramatic personal contrast between the two main characters of this drama? Jairus is a man with power and respect throughout the community. He comes to us with a name, a status, and a household. The bleeding woman has nothing but pain, shame, and poverty. Their differences could not be more stark.

From a typical human perspective, Jairus should hold Jesus' attention. And yet Jesus will not be rushed through the crowd because of Jairus's social status. Now that this story has taken an unexpected and dramatic turn toward this impoverished, unclean, destitute woman, now that Jesus has affirmed her as a faithful daughter, Mark might want us to wonder what will happen to Jairus, the synagogue leader. What if Jesus now intends to turn the tables? She was oppressed. She was powerless. Jairus represents everything that made her situation worse. He represents rejection from community and care. What if Jairus will now be the recipient of the type of shame this woman has endured? What if he will be cut off, just as she has been excluded from the community he leads? What if he will lose what is precious to him—his own daughter— just as this woman has lost everything in her desperate search for healing?

Sure enough, in the midst of Jesus' words to the woman, men from Jairus's household approach. "Your daughter is dead," they tell him. "Why bother the teacher anymore?"

This woman reached out to Jesus for healing and received it immediately. From the vantage point of the servants, for Jairus's daughter, it has been in vain.

When I've read this story in the past, I've often imagined myself as the bleeding woman. I see myself as one who comes to Jesus with shame and fear and desperation. I see myself as one who needs healing in my body and spirit and community. I think back to myself as a girl in a hospital with a paralyzed stomach. I think of how deeply I identify with our daughter Penny and the ways that being a family affected by disability moves us to a place of social disadvantage. I have never identified with Jairus.

Yet I wonder whether Jairus is the more apt comparison. I have wealth and education. I carry with me my pale skin and European heritage and all the benefits that our culture gives me because of these attributes. Even more, I attended seminary. I speak and write and teach and lead from a position of religious authority. If I uncritically absorb the message of Flannery O'Connor, or of theologians who write about how Jesus shows a "preferential option for the poor," or of activists who call white people in to start listening and stop centering themselves, or of writers who tell me that the schools I went to are built on exclusion and privilege and should be eradicated, then perhaps I will imagine that Jesus—champion of the marginalized and outcast—wants to rebuke me. Or, to soften it a bit, perhaps I will imagine Jesus doesn't have time for me. I have enough resources already. Enough social support. Enough.

Jesus makes Jairus wait, but Jesus does not rebuke Jairus. Jesus sends this woman into her community with words of blessing, then turns his attention back to this anxious father and continues on his healing journey. Mark writes, "Overhearing what they said, Jesus told [the synagogue leader], 'Don't be afraid; just believe'" (Mark 5:36).

Jairus is like Mrs. Turpin. He has to decide whether he is willing to take his place at the end of the line. Whether he can see the points of connection between himself and this bleeding woman. Whether he can bear the public humiliation of waiting, the fear and grief of wondering what has happened to his daughter while he was away, and the insecurity and uncertainty of walking with Jesus to his home now that he has heard news of his daughter's death.

When Jesus resumes his walk with Jairus, he shows us that healing is for everyone. For rich and poor. Female and male. Able and disabled. Those on the margins and those at the center. The powerful and the powerless.

We all need healing from Jesus. And Jesus' healing is for all of us.

As much as Mark draws attention to the contrast between Jairus and this woman, he also highlights what they have in common. It is in their commonality that we begin to understand what we all need in order to receive healing. There are the overt connections: The woman has been bleeding for twelve years; Jairus's child is twelve years old. The woman is called *Daughter* by Jesus; Jairus has come to Jesus on behalf of his own beloved daughter. But there is another set of more subtle comparisons between these two figures. Both Jairus and this woman have come to the end of their ability to solve their own problem. They come to Jesus out of a desperate need. They both reach out to him for help. And finally, they respond to his instructions. They acknowledge need, ask for help, and respond.

I grew up in a churchgoing household. As a child, I knelt by my bed to say prayers most nights and went to vacation Bible school in the summer and memorized the Twenty-Third Psalm in Sunday school. In middle school, I wore a white robe for my official confirmation and prayed with the elders of the church. I was always responsible and nice and well-behaved.

I went away to boarding school when I was thirteen years old. It was only an hour from home, but it still represented a moment when I began choosing for myself whether I went to church on Sunday morning (I didn't) or read the Bible or prayed on my own (nope) or believed what I had been taught about God (I wasn't sure). I got good grades. I worked hard. I was similar to all the other earnest, wealthy, mostly white kids at my school. I didn't have time for religion. I didn't feel a need for Jesus.

But when I got sick the following year, when I lost the lead in the play, and my grades were in jeopardy, and I left school and stared at the wall while hooked up to an IV of fats and fluids at Yale New Haven hospital, I knew I was needy. For the first time, I couldn't ignore my own sense of helplessness. I wasn't sure that Jesus was the answer. I just knew I needed something and that the world of achievement and perfection and accolades and wealth and whiteness had failed me. Or I had failed it. All eighty-seven pounds of me.

Over a decade later, when I sat in another hospital bed holding our baby girl in my arms, looking at her round cheeks and long eyelashes, feeling the gentle exhale of her breath, feeling the tears trickle down my face with fear and doubt and guilt and grief because she had been diagnosed with Down syndrome, that world of achievement and expectation failed me once again.

And then there were the years of quotidian needs, when our kids were toddlers and I needed more sleep and more companionship and, once more, permission not to sprint on the treadmill of productivity.

In all these times of need, and in so many of the intervening moments of desperation and grief and anger and shame, I cried out to God. It is here that I find myself both in the bleeding woman and in Jairus. They both fall at Jesus' feet, desperate for help. They've both exhausted the other options. They know they are needy, and they turn to Jesus as their only hope.

It's hard for humans to acknowledge our neediness and ask for help. Jesus tells us it's even harder for rich people and people in positions of power. He tells the story of a rich fool who didn't recognize his need for God and instead stored up human possessions, thinking they would be his salvation (Luke 12:13–21). He talks about a rich man who is condemned to suffer in hell after he fails to help the poor while alive (Luke 16:19–31). Jesus looks with compassion on a rich man who cannot bear to part with his wealth. He tells his disciples that it is virtually impossible—harder than a camel going through the eye of a needle—for the rich to inherit the kingdom of heaven (Mark 10:17–27). Two thousand years ago, as now, people with power and wealth could easily deny the neediness inherent in their humanity.

Still, with all the warnings about the problems of riches, Jesus also attracts rich followers, and he doesn't ask all of them to give away their possessions. He dines in their homes and enjoys banquets among them. He celebrates with them. He tells parables in which he compares God to rich landowners.[4] It's not the riches themselves that get in the way of the kingdom of heaven. It's the inability to acknowledge need, to ask for help, and to respond in faith to whatever Jesus commands, even and especially if that means divesting themselves of riches. People who live on the brink of poverty—as the vast majority of people in Jesus' world did—have a far greater understanding of the precarity and vulnerability of their lives than those who experience material security and stability.

But Jairus understands his need. Jairus loves his daughter more than he loves his position in the community, more than he loves what other people think of him, more than he loves his religious ideology that would have said this radical rabbi named Jesus was a reprobate. In his need, Jairus turns to Jesus.

Grade point averages and bank statements papered over my own sense of need until I found myself in the hospital and just couldn't deny it any more. Like Jairus, I desperately needed help, and though I wasn't entirely sure what I believed, I too sought that help in Jesus.

Jairus walks with Jesus from the shores of the lake through the crowded streets. He pauses to witness a miracle. But that same miracle delays Jesus' arrival at Jairus's home and seems to cost Jairus his daughter's life. Yet when Jesus turns back to Jairus, it is not with words of rebuke or resignation, but with words of hope: "Just believe." Jesus walks with Jairus and enters the room of his little girl, who has died from her illness. And, Mark reports, Jairus witnesses another miracle as Jesus "took her by the hand and said to her, '*Talitha Koum!*' (which means, 'Little girl, I say to you, get up!')" (Mark 5:41).[5] His daughter rises from her deathbed.

Mark weaves these two stories together both to draw out the contrast and to connect them. Jesus' healing is for the whole of humanity, from the poorest woman to the richest man. Those on the margins and those in the center. Straight people and gay people. Democrats and Republicans. Believers and atheists. Oppressed and oppressor.

Jesus' healing is available for all.

PART II

Barriers to Healing

CHAPTER 6

The Barrier
of Distraction

When Jesus had again crossed over by boat to the other side of the lake, a large crowd gathered around him while he was by the lake. Then one of the synagogue leaders, named Jairus, came, and when he saw Jesus, he fell at his feet. He pleaded earnestly with him, "My little daughter is dying. Please come and put your hands on her so that she will be healed and live." So Jesus went with him.

A large crowd followed and pressed around him.

—MARK 5:21–24

When our kids were all out of diapers, we took our first family vacation. It was a beautiful trip—clear skies, blue water, white sandy beaches. We stayed at a resort that offered a "kids' club" in the morning, so I had time for walks by myself and with Peter, for naps in the shade of a palm tree, for times of prayer, for reading lots of books. It was extravagant and luxurious. It also involved a daily struggle over where we should spend the afternoon.

Every day after kids' club, our children wanted to go to the pool. They wanted to jump into the chlorinated water, dive for rings, and then get a Shirley Temple at the poolside bar. Every day, we tried instead to cajole them toward the ocean, the feeling of sand between their toes, the sight of hermit crabs scuttling across the beach, the pulsing rhythm of the waves. That vast expanse of water requiring our respect and our attention with its power, its constant swelling motion. The ocean, filled with rocks and coral, teeming with life. The ocean, unpredictable and a little scary. Every day, we led them toward the depths, and they wanted to go back to the pool.

The pool didn't challenge them. It didn't invite them to overcome fear. They never left our time there with a sense of adventure or wonder. But it was safe, and fun, and immediately gratifying.

That struggle between the pool and the ocean feels like a metaphor for my own life. I stay in my safe, entertaining, controlled environment in any number of ways. I scroll through Instagram instead of connecting with a friend. I rush through each week with a relentless to-do list instead of saying no to a few things and enjoying some rest. I run on a treadmill instead of snapping on my snowshoes and getting cold and wet and experiencing the glory of the landscape after a winter storm. I've spent lots of time in the "swimming pool" of life.

My life in the shallows starts as soon as I wake up. I roll over in the dark and reach for my phone. Before I've even gotten dressed or made a cup of tea or taken a few minutes to pray, I've already scanned the day's headlines, scrolled through email and social media, and replied to a few text messages. I can argue that I'm being efficient or that all these messages and news reports keep me engaged with the world. But really I'm filling my mind with information from the moment my eyes open. Instead of entering into the stillness of the morning, which might mean facing my own restlessness and discontent and regret, I'm turning on a switch in my brain that commends me for efficiency and productivity. That switch stays on, with my phone close at hand, all day long.

Every few months, I impose some sort of limit on my phone usage in general and on the early morning phone situation in particular. I decide I'll place my phone downstairs before I head up to bed and I won't look at it again until after I've spent time with God. Or I decide I'll create a setting that puts the phone in airplane mode until seven in the morning. Once, in a burst of self-improvement energy, I decided to remove all social media, email, and news apps from my phone for a thirty-day digital detox. (Thank you, Cal Newport.[1]) I didn't come close to thirty days, but through the week or so that I lasted, I found myself gazing plaintively at the weather during most free moments. I had kept WeatherBug on the phone, because who would be tempted by a weather app? But there I was, standing in line at the grocery store and scrolling through the ten-day forecast. There I was, sitting on the toilet and wondering whether our thermometer would agree with the hourly temperature predictions. I studied the maps—lightning strikes, pollen count, precipitation. I became curious about storms in the Midwest and drought in Colorado.

My attempt to take away distraction only proved how distractible I am.

I am not here to write a treatise on digital distraction, nor am I here to dictate how or whether to limit the role these devices have in our lives. But I do want to ask myself why I allow my phone, and all that it represents, to keep me from listening to the voice of God.

I think back to when William was an infant. He woke up a lot in the night. And as much as I cursed the sleepless nature of those early months, they also beckoned me into a rhythm of prayer. As I sat in the rocker and nursed him, I traveled with him in my heart from his bedroom down the hallway to where Penny and Peter lay asleep. Then to other parts of the Northeast—my parents, my sisters, my grandparents. I prayed for friends in New York and New Jersey, Richmond, Los Angeles, Denver. I prayed for people I had heard about on the news who were suffering in some way. I prayed for our church and school and community.

Three years later, when Marilee was born, I planned to resume that practice of midnight prayer. But then, when she cried out, I brought my phone with me. I scrolled through the *New York Times* headlines and read emails instead. And now, on many a lovely quiet morning with my cup of tea and journal, I begin my day not with the gentle whisper of the Spirit of God but with the flashing lights of commerce and information and getting things done. I bemoan the fact that social media companies studied casinos in order to create entertainment systems that hook my attention. And then I come back for more.

Earlier this year, I told a praying friend that I wanted to listen for God's voice in my life. She suggested that I might choose to intentionally refrain from podcasts, audiobooks, and the radio. It seemed like a good idea, so I decided to "fast" from listening to the media in order to allow more listening to God. I gritted my teeth through a few days of silence. I quickly returned to the noise. When I'm driving, doing mundane household tasks, brushing my teeth, walking from room to room—I consume information. I fill my mind with facts and ideas that range from trivial and meaningless to profound. All this data distracts me from the voice of my own inner critic. It distracts me from feelings of boredom or anxiety or loneliness. This little glowing rectangle also distracts me from the people who matter most—Peter and our children. And it distracts me from God. It keeps me from the deeper work that might transform that inner critic and address those feelings and bring healing.

Spiritual director and author Ruth Haley Barton writes about how the soul—that inner, true self, that shy, skittish part of ourselves that can tell us what we are feeling, what hurts, what brings us joy, what matters most—is like a deer in the forest. Timid. Cautious. Waiting for a quiet moment to emerge.[2] When I fill all the crevices of time in my life with noise and information, I crowd out my soul. I crowd out the opportunity to listen to God. I avoid the pain of admitting my fears and hurts and failings. I crowd out the invitation to be made well.

Although we live two thousand years after the disciples and the bleeding woman and Jairus, even though we live in a world of broadband internet connections and satellites in outer space and the capability for nuclear war, we aren't that different from the people in Jesus' day. Like them, we need to be made well. Like them, we encounter barriers to healing, and one of those barriers is that of distraction. We keep ourselves busy with thoughts and tasks and desires and entertainment in order to keep ourselves from the discomfort and pain of confronting our hurts and admitting our neediness.

Jairus was a rare wealthy and powerful person who approached Jesus with a sense of humility and need. For him, the likelihood of death for his daughter overcame any sense of invincibility or self-sufficiency. He—like the bleeding woman, the tax collectors, the sinful woman, the fishermen, and the political radicals who followed Jesus—acknowledged his helplessness and turned to Jesus for help.

In our modern era, many of us live with enough wealth, power, and comfort to ignore or deny our neediness. We pretend that we are healthy and well. We maintain our physical fitness through health coach apps and Beachbody exercise plans. We try a new kitchen gadget or subscribe to a meal kit for preparing healthy food. We put more and more money toward the "wellness" industry, and then we don't transform our bodies or experience the freedom from pain we wanted. But Jesus offered more than a miracle to the people he healed back then, and he wants more than a superficial vision of health for us now. Jesus cares about alleviating our pain, but Jesus doesn't care about flat abs or wrinkle-free foreheads. And he knows that addressing bodily pain also means addressing everything beneath the surface—our broken spirits and wounded hearts and fragile relationships.

To live in God's healing presence is like swimming in the ocean. Immense. Frightening. Powerful. Beautiful. Where, as the psalmist writes, "deep calls to deep" (Psalm 42:7). Where answers don't come easily. Where pain is exposed rather than covered over. Where healing leads to transformation.

We live in a world where it is easy to avoid the hard questions, to ignore our own selfishness, to fill our days with busy but meaningless activity. Deep calls out to deep, but sometimes I long to stay shallow. Whether it's food, chitchat, hours on Instagram, working long days, or watching mindless television, we have constructed countless ways to avoid looking at the brokenness within our souls. Again, Ruth Haley Barton names the spiritual consequences of distraction: "One of the dangers of living in a constant state of distraction is that we never go to the bottom of our pain, our sadness, our emptiness, which means we never find that rock-bottom place of the peace that passes understanding and rest ourselves there."[3]

Although the people in Jesus' day didn't have smartphones, it was still easy to become distracted and miss Jesus' invitation to healing. Throughout Mark's gospel, the crowds represent the danger of distraction. In this story of Jairus and the bleeding woman, Mark tells us that the crowds "pressed against" Jesus. Mark portrays the crowds as a physical and psychological threat. Luke also uses ominous language to describe the crowds. In his version of this story, Luke writes that the crowds "choke" Jesus when he gets off the boat and starts to walk with Jairus. Both Mark and Luke use language that invites us as readers to consider what "crowds" us from seeing what Jesus is doing, what keeps us from receiving Jesus' healing touch, what holds us on the surface instead of inviting us to the depths.

Luke uses this word *choke* in only one other passage in his narrative. It comes a few paragraphs earlier, where Jesus describes people who start to grow in their knowledge of God and become "choked" by worries and pleasures (Luke 8:14). Jesus envisions a young plant that begins to grow toward the light but gets cut off, stifled by thorns. When Luke uses this unusual word, *choked*, to describe both what happens to that plant and then what happens to Jesus, he invites us to connect the two. Just as the crowds of people threaten to "choke" Jesus and impede his healing work, so the worries and the pleasures of this life threaten to crowd out Jesus in each of us.

I've read about large crowds at stadiums and sporting events where people get trampled underfoot. These deaths are entirely unintentional. In these situations, we are often unaware of the danger, even if it is imminent. Luke uses a violent image—of strangling the life of a plant—to hint at not only the physical danger that the crowd poses but also the spiritual danger. Jesus tells his followers that worries and pleasures can choke us from experiencing the flourishing life God has for us, and all without our even being aware of the threat. How much more so today, in our age of instant gratification and iPhones and twenty-four-hour work cycles? Long before the digital age, Jesus knew some people would hear his message and love what he had to say. He also knew we might start to grow and then be stunted. Like my kids, whose growth gets crowded out by entertainment and sugar. Like me, cut off from knowing God better by information and productivity. By Netflix and home decorating and bills to pay.

When I return to this interaction between Jairus and Jesus, I see the ominous form the crowd takes, the way the crowd threatens to impede Jesus from offering healing. It all leads me to ask, Am I allowing Jesus' healing to be "choked" out of my life? Am I distracting myself from the invitation to be healed? Instead of confronting why I snapped at Marilee or why I'm afraid I'll miss a deadline or why I'm sad after a family gathering, I can turn to my phone. We live in a time when the distractions, worries, and pleasures of our lives keep us detached from need, keep us from being made well.

The phone helps me remain on the surface of life, but it isn't my only way to avoid attending to the deeper cry for healing within my soul. I also have a habitual return to chardonnay. Chardonnay does a lovely job of dulling the sharp edges of any pain I feel. *Pour a glass of golden numbness and just keep getting things done.* It keeps me distracted from discomfort, boredom, exhaustion. But staying distracted from pain also means staying distracted from healing.

I first noticed how I used alcohol as a distraction from my emotions nine years ago, after we moved with three little ones and I found myself bored and irritated and angry and feeling guilty about it. I've written before about what I now call "my year of wine and nachos." After that year, I cut back on alcohol. I started seeing Anne, experienced that healing from back pain, changed my eating habits, and started exercising regularly again. It began a virtuous spiral toward health and well-being.

But when the COVID-19 pandemic hit, I—like many of my fellow Americans, especially moms with kids at home—found myself back in that place of desperation. In March of 2020, I more or less lost my job. All my upcoming speaking events were canceled. I was writing an essay for the *New York Times*, and my editor stopped writing me back. I received a rejection from a master's program, and another rejection from a church. Peter's job became only more challenging now that he needed to lead hundreds of frightened faculty and parents through a crisis while he ran an academic institution with teenagers from all over the globe. And all three of our kids were at home, indefinitely. Marilee, age nine, had no assigned schoolwork. We were encouraged to make crafts and explore nature together. Meanwhile, it was pretty clear that Penny would not learn much without supervision. William seemed to be receiving enough relevant instruction from his teachers to therefore be in danger of total neglect from Peter and me. By that June, I hadn't resumed the nachos, but large and multiple glasses of wine were a regular way of life. According to news reports, I was not alone in choosing the route of self-medication to handle my woes. Alcohol use was up by all measures during the pandemic, and the days on which women reported "heavy drinking" increased by 41 percent.[4]

These are my crowds—information, productivity, and alcohol. These are the ways I stay on the surface. These are the things that threaten to choke me and lure my attention away from the healing that Jesus offers. I'm sure some people use the same distractions as I do, while others numb with entertainment or shopping or overworking or overeating or overexercising. But almost all of us distract ourselves from admitting our pain and hurt and fear. Almost all of us try to crowd out the vulnerability of feeling needy, dependent, and helpless before God.

Making ourselves available to the loving, healing work of God means making ourselves vulnerable. The word *vulnerable*, at its root, means "able to be wounded." It's ironic—in order to be healed, we need to allow the possibility that we will be wounded. We need to lay down the armor of distraction and come to God as we are. Like the bleeding woman, like Jairus, falling at Jesus' feet. Both of them ignored the crowd. Both of them paid attention to Jesus.

Jairus and the bleeding woman offer me hope. Overcoming the crowds does not mean muscling their way through or gaining a private audience with Jesus. It simply means putting their attention on Jesus himself. They both literally fall at his feet, which brings their gaze to him alone. Jesus takes a posture with them that implies he, too, narrows his vision and his attention and sees them in their fullness.

I don't need to conquer my distractions in order to come to Jesus. I do need to turn my fragmented attention to him. And so, even with my iPhone nearby, even with my to-do list threatening to choke out any space for the Spirit, even on a morning after consuming more alcohol than I wanted to the night before, even then, I am invited to return to God's healing presence. In the midst of the choking crowds, Jesus heals the bleeding woman. He heals Jairus's daughter. He can heal us too.

CHAPTER 7

The Barrier of Shame

Then the woman, knowing what had happened to her, came and fell at his feet, and trembling with fear, told him the whole truth...
—MARK 5:33

One summer when my sister Brooks was twelve years old, she got a splinter while running on a deck in bare feet. Even after she extracted a sizable piece of wood, her heel hurt so much she couldn't walk. My mother took her to the doctor, who looked at Brooks's foot and couldn't detect any reason for the pain. He sent them home. Brooks knew that something was very wrong, so she took some tweezers and opened up the place where her foot hurt. For days, she picked and picked and picked at it until she was able to extract a thick splinter about an inch long that had pierced her heel so perfectly and deeply it wasn't even visible on the outside. She created a new wound in order to get at the deeper problem of the splinter that was wedged inside her heel. When she removed it, she caused herself more immediate pain. But with that release, she opened up a way for healing to begin.

We all still squirm when Brooks tells that story. But I return to it because it stands as a visceral reminder of what happens when we don't pursue the healing we need. There are countless ways our bodies and our spirits tell us that all is not well. We break out in hives or start having migraines or back pain or gastrointestinal distress. We wake up in the middle of the night with our mind racing around the track of responsibility. We find ourselves unable to pray because we feel so distracted by our thoughts. Instead of exposing the source of the pain so that we can open up a path for healing, we try to cover it. Instead of persisting in digging out the problem, we hope that a Band-Aid will do the trick. Whether through alcohol or Netflix or shopping or ice cream or getting things done, we numb our pain, ignore it, or deny it instead of exposing the wound and inviting the healing.

When I asked Brooks to confirm my recollection of the splinter incident, she texted me, "Yes. I could feel it but not see it because of how deep it was." Her words felt like another portrait of pain writ large. Our bodies and emotions send out signals to tell us about wounds that need tending, but so often we ignore those signals because we cannot see, or bear to see, their source. The pain is too deep for us even to acknowledge it. And so we limp along through our days.

We live in a culture that is afraid of pain, afraid of disease and suffering and death. We have moved our cemeteries to the outskirts of town and sequestered older members of our society. We treat aging as shameful instead of honorable. We dye our hair and spend billions of dollars a year on antiaging creams and treatments.[1] We use pain medications in record numbers. And despite these attempts to avoid, deny, and numb pain, the CDC reports that fifty million Americans suffer from chronic physical pain. Another report finds that roughly 20 percent of the population struggles with an anxiety disorder—a type of mental pain. We can only imagine the millions more whose daily experience of anxiety goes unreported. In yet another study, the CDC reports that around 10 percent of women and five percent of men in America suffer from depression.[2] Whether our pain is physical or emotional, as a society, we are experiencing a lot of it.

The good news is that Jesus is not afraid of this pain. When he encounters the bleeding woman, Jesus immediately knows that power has gone out from him, even though he doesn't know where that power has gone. He insists on coming face-to-face with whomever touched him. He refuses to ignore or deny this woman or her pain. Rather, Jesus moves toward her, just as he moves toward us in our needy, vulnerable, broken state.

Jesus' approach to healing this woman runs parallel with the dozens of other encounters he has with people in need. Take, for example, the story in John 5, where Jesus goes to Jerusalem for a feast. He is not in the city for a mission trip. He is not there in response to a natural disaster. To get a better idea of what Jesus is doing, we can imagine ourselves on the way to Thanksgiving dinner at Grandma's house. We're all dressed up; the green bean casserole is warm in the trunk under some tinfoil. Our destination is clear. Similarly, Jesus is on his way to the temple to celebrate a religious festival. But when Jesus approaches Jerusalem, he doesn't go directly to the temple. Instead, he stops at the pool of Bethesda, a place where he knows the sick gather in hopes of healing. Jesus shows up at what equates to an outdoor field hospital, with masses of hurting people holding on to the faint hope of touching what is rumored to be healing water. Jesus approaches this large group of people in pain, and without any fanfare or introduction, he talks to a man who has been "an invalid" for thirty-eight years. Jesus walks right up to him and asks, "Do you want to get well?" (v. 6).

I used to think that the man is making an excuse for himself when he replies, "I have no one to help me into the pool when the water is stirred" (v. 7). But it's also possible he's just stating the truth in response to this stranger's impertinent question: *Isn't it obvious? I'm doing the best I can. I desperately want to be made well. But I'm stuck here with a not-so-great plan for how I might possibly be healed.*

The man is all alone. He's sick. He's gotten as close as he can to the best solution he can think of for his problem, much like the bleeding woman who spent all she had on doctors. But once this man tells Jesus his situation, Jesus instructs him to stand up, take his mat, and walk. The man obeys, and he finds himself unexpectedly on his feet, healed, like the bleeding woman, through the power of this stranger.

Jesus knows nothing of this man's—or the bleeding woman's—worthiness or devotion. He doesn't ask either of them to demonstrate knowledge of the Scriptures. He doesn't require prayer or sacrifice. He just wants to know if this man wants to be made well, and as soon as the man gives the slightest indication that the answer is yes, Jesus acts on his behalf.

If we give Jesus an inch, he will take a mile.

Jesus is not afraid of our pain or our neediness. Nor is he put off by our sin or our shame. Jesus moves toward us in our pain, our isolation, our meager and ineffective attempts to find relief on our own. Jesus longs to heal us.

So what keeps us from getting well?

I think back to my own ongoing experience of healing. I used to seek relief for pain and illness only through physical measures: Advil for the aching back, Tylenol PM for the sleep-lessness, antibiotics for the sinus infections. It's not that these medical measures were bad. Modern medicine, whether in the form of antidepressants or antibiotics, can play a crucial role in healing. But this solution was simply, and especially over the course of time, not enough. Treating medication as an end point was my way of ignoring, denying, and rejecting the notion that my body was warning me of pain within my soul that I had not yet addressed. And much as the medication held illness and physical pain at bay, I could not heal that inner pain on my own or with dozens of doctor's visits. I needed the healing love of God.

It took a lot for me to receive that healing love. Even once I had exhausted medical solutions, and even after friends and family commented on how surprising it was that I got sick so often, even then I resisted looking at my illness and pain through an emotional or spiritual lens. I didn't want to expose the wounds that needed deeper healing. I told myself I didn't have the time. I said it wasn't important enough to warrant my attention. The truth is, I was afraid of what a deeper self-investigation might reveal.

I wonder if, like me, the bleeding woman felt afraid of what healing might entail. It may not be fair to even make the comparison. Surely her suffering was greater than mine and compounded by the social stigma surrounding her particular affliction. She had far fewer resources than I to try to address her needs. Still, Mark tells us that she looked for solutions in all sorts of places until eventually—desperate but brave—she turned to Jesus.

Once we confront the surface level of distraction—once we begin to ignore the "crowds" and turn our attention to Jesus—then Jesus begins to address that deeper level of healing needed within our souls. It is at this point that shame tries to cover over our wounds and protect us from the pain of exposure. Bestselling author and shame researcher Brené Brown writes, "Shame is the intensely painful feeling or experience of believing that we are flawed and therefore unworthy of love and belonging."[3] Brown also writes that shame is universal. Every human being struggles with a sense of shame, this feeling that is as ancient as Adam and Eve covering their nakedness in the garden of Eden.

The bleeding woman's encounter with the healing presence of Jesus encapsulates the ways that shame tries to keep us from experiencing God's healing love. Yes, the woman is bold enough to reach out through the crowd for Jesus' robe. But then she almost forfeits the holistic healing Jesus wants to offer. She almost slips away from him once she feels that her bleeding has stopped. Even after he calls her out, she tries to hide. When she finally comes forward, she does so with fear. Shame keeps her from approaching Jesus. Shame similarly keeps many of us from exposing the woundedness within our souls. Two millennia later, shame still gets in the way of receiving God's healing love in our lives.

Brené Brown's research shows that shame causes us to internalize the thought that we are not good enough, and we never will be. The bleeding woman had internalized her own culture's messages of shame. Her bleeding rendered her unclean and cut off from worship. She also lived in a culture in which illness was often conflated with sinfulness. And her illness rendered her infertile. She couldn't live up to cultural expectations that she bear children. She could never be good enough.

For different reasons, I also internalized messages along the way that told me I could never be good enough. As a kid, I learned that I like books too much to ever be cool enough to have lots of friends. As a sister, I heard a message that I was too religious to become a confidant. As a wife, I told myself I wasn't athletic or outgoing enough to be a good spouse of the head of school. As a woman, I've felt that I don't care enough about home decorating and appearance to measure up to my peers. And I haven't worked full-time since our kids were born. Not good enough. Not good enough. Not good enough.

I didn't recognize all those internalized messages of shame until I began to notice the pain and illness in my body that recurred without warning.

For me, to seek deeper healing meant looking not at the surface level of pain but at the deeper layers, the years of dysfunctional patterns, the lies I have told myself about myself. It meant noticing habits of sin and neglect and denial. It meant naming shame for what it was. It meant digging up hurt from my past in order to expose that hurt to love. It meant a deeper level of vulnerability before God. It meant coming face-to-face with Jesus rather than slipping away in the crowd.

Over many years, as I have experienced deeper intimacy with God, I have nevertheless continued to resist admitting my need for God's healing. Take the moment when I developed an itchy red patch just below my left eyelid. By this point, I had spent enough time thinking about how our bodies communicate with us to wonder whether this sudden and unexplained redness might indicate some sort of disconnect between my body and my soul. I thought redness around the eyes might well signal irritation with what I see inside myself. It was the summer of 2020, the year that revealed to many of us truths we would rather not see. For me, five months into the COVID-19 pandemic, top of the list was not being able to accomplish much in the midst of supervising our kids' at-home learning. But just below that surface agitation, there was that long list of accusations I had absorbed from family and culture that told me I would never be good enough in any of my endeavors. And there was guilt over my sense of hardship, when I knew my experience of this global pandemic was both far easier and far more protected than that of billions of other people. There was the additional shame I felt over the five pounds that had crept onto my middle while filling this role of full-time household manager and opening yet another bottle of chardonnay.

I didn't want to look inward and acknowledge my anger about my circumstances or about my behavior. I didn't want to seek out a therapist and talk about my problems. I didn't want to invite God's healing presence into the shame and fear and despair I felt about what was on the horizon. As Curt Thompson, author of *The Soul of Shame*, writes, "Healing [from shame] always requires vulnerability and exposure of all our wounded parts."[4] I didn't want any more exposure.

So instead of addressing shame, I went to the dermatologist. She took one look at my eye and diagnosed me with something that involved a long acronym. She prescribed a topical cream, which did indeed alleviate the redness and the itchiness within a few days. I am grateful for that relief. But I also was struck by the inadequacy of this solution. The doctor didn't diagnose me with shame, but when I asked her the cause, she said, "Oh. This is stress-related." Rather than suggest I take a look at the root cause of my irritated skin, she gave me a way to hide the visible manifestation of that stress with a topical cream. It was easy to resume my daily life without doing anything to address the source of the problem itself.

Psychiatrist Bessel van der Kolk writes about the role of medication in healing. He affirms that with many of his psychiatric patients, he prescribes antidepressants and other drugs in order to arrest psychotic or depressive symptoms. He also writes that these medications never heal the pain. They simply alleviate it enough to open up a space for the deeper healing to begin. Medication is often necessary, but insufficient, for healing.[5]

When I look closely at my life, I notice a pattern of addressing physical symptoms without addressing underlying stress or emotions. Take a Claritin for a sneezing fit rather than trace the mental map of anxiety to its starting point. Drink alcohol instead of feeling the pain of rejection. Scroll through Instagram instead of entering God's presence with all my jumbled thoughts and feelings.

As it nearly did for the bleeding woman, shame keeps many of us from coming face-to-face with Jesus. To receive the healing love of Jesus means to uncover our wounds, to lay bare our intimate desires, hopes, dreams, failures, and fears. For the bleeding woman, this exposure involved falling on her knees in front of a crowd and admitting that she had dared to touch Jesus. For me, it has meant many years of reflection on when and why I become irritated with our kids, when and why I berate myself, when and why I turn to coping mechanisms instead of to God. It has meant admitting that I tried to achieve love through performance rather than believing I am loved for who I am already. It has meant countering the lies that so easily dominate my thinking, the lies that tell me I am not, and never will be, good enough. It has meant doing the work of finding, at various points, a therapist, a spiritual director, and a group of trusted friends who will listen to me and challenge me and hold me up in prayer.

So much of our cultural imagery around God as an angry and patriarchal deity offers an impression that it would never be safe to bring our vulnerable and wounded selves into God's presence. Just like the bleeding woman, trembling in fear, we will never approach God with our needs unless we have confidence that God is a safe and loving agent of healing.

A few years ago, I had an experience that gave me a tangible understanding of what it might mean to come to God with our wounded bodies and souls and ask God to heal us. My friend Ashley broke her neck and collarbone in a mountain biking accident. She came within millimeters of severing her spinal column at the base of her neck. She avoided paralysis and death, but her injuries were severe. After her surgery, I flew to Nashville to stay with her for a few days as her husband went back to work. One afternoon, she asked if I could help her take a shower.

She removed the brace stabilizing her neck and the sling holding her collarbone in place. I turned on the faucet. Her job now was to sit motionless while I poured water over her body and washed her clean.

I don't know what it took for her to be able to sit in such a posture of vulnerability with me. I do know that her accident had brought her face-to-face with her need, and that even amid the pain and discomfort of her healing, she felt overwhelmed with gratitude that she was alive and moving. She trusted me enough to bring me this very simple but real need, and I could not have felt more honored to receive that trust.

Ashley was young and beautiful. She had no visible wounds. But it was still a vulnerable moment when she exposed her broken body to my care. Similarly, we are invited to bring our dirty and wounded souls to God, that we might be washed clean. In the Old Testament, Isaiah announces that God will wash us "white as snow" (Isaiah 1:18). King David pleads with God to "wash away all my iniquity and cleanse me from my sin" (Psalm 51:2). The New Testament writers emphasize the cleansing waters of baptism. Jesus stoops down and takes the posture of a servant as he washes his disciples' dirty feet on the night before his death (John 13:1–17). I can only imagine what the woman who had been bleeding for twelve years looked and smelled like. And I can only imagine the gentle care Jesus offered as he placed his hands upon her,[6] called her *Daughter*, and made her well.

Cleansing, healing—from sin, from shame, from fear—all of this is available to us when we come, even when we come trembling, to Jesus.

For me to admit my need for healing is to take off my armor and enter into that vulnerability. For me to come forward rather than try to slip away in the crowd is to acknowledge the places where I am dirty and smelly and wounded and allow them to be exposed. And then, it is to receive the love available to cleanse and heal me.

In the midst of what sometimes feels like a never-ending quest to be made well, I am heartened by the reality that Jesus doesn't wait for us to overcome the barriers to healing. The man lying by the pool doesn't give Jesus a full answer to whether he wants to get well, and Jesus heals him anyway. The bleeding woman would have settled for a little bit of healing instead of everything Jesus wanted to offer her. We, too, are invited to come, again and again and again, with our fear and our shame, our sin and our need, to receive the healing love of God.

CHAPTER 8

The Barrier of Anxiety

While Jesus was still speaking, some people came from the house of Jairus, the synagogue leader. "Your daughter is dead," they said. "Why bother the teacher anymore?"

Overhearing what they said, Jesus told him, "Don't be afraid; just believe."

—MARK 5:35–36

I wasn't worried when I first heard about COVID-19. For those early months of 2020, it seemed like a distant and abstract problem. I kept reminding myself that the flu kills tens of thousands of people every year, and I had never registered it as a major threat. I thought about all the ways our modern culture invites us to experience anxiety. The alerts and alarms in cars flashing danger at every turn. The headlines suggesting that every storm could be catastrophic. The product labels warning about death by choking, swallowing, suffocation. I figured COVID-19 would be similar: a big-deal news story with red alerts that would soon enough become as irrelevant as the fear that the world would end at midnight at the start of the year 2000.

But by early March, hospitals in Italy were overwhelmed. It became clear that COVID-19 had made its way to the United States. I started bumping elbows with friends instead of offering a hug in greeting. We made little self-deprecating jokes about standing six feet apart. We wondered if our kids might be out of school for a few weeks. Then William's church service trip was canceled. Our plans to take the girls into Manhattan for the day were postponed indefinitely. The stock market plummeted. Schools began to close. Peter began fielding emergency response calls daily with other heads of school all trying to decide whether to allow students back on campus for the spring term. I still wasn't worried.

Or at least that's what I told myself. I made a plan for the few weeks we would be at home. We got together with friends for walks outside. We created lists of activities to inspire the children not to default to screens at every turn. When I looked to the future, I reassured myself that we would be back in school shortly, that my parents would not contract the virus, and that the rest of us were young and healthy and didn't need to be afraid.

Then we received word that our kids would not return to school in person that year. That summer camp was canceled. That indoor gatherings were unlikely to be safe, indefinitely. That kids would miss out on graduations and sports seasons. That adults would postpone weddings. That millions of people had lost their jobs. That lines for food banks and emergency support stretched through parking lots and city blocks. That hundreds of thousands of Americans and millions of people around the globe would die.

I had it relatively easy. Still, the work of "pushing our family up the happy hill," as one of my friends blithely named it, was exhausting. My descent into drinking copious amounts of wine began. Many evenings all five of us retreated to our various corners of the house, with screens at the ready.

One morning that spring, I woke up feeling as though my back had been replaced by a plank of wood. This wasn't the generic lower-back ache I'd experienced before. This wasn't a rubber band stretched too tight for comfort or a lumpy sweater with a few knots to work out. My back felt like a flat board that might crack if I moved the wrong way.

That same week, one friend texted me that she was in bed because she had thrown her back out. My sister called and said, "I'm walking instead of running because I did something to my back." My own running partner canceled because she said she needed to see the chiropractor, who, of course, was not allowed to see patients at that time. Peter started massaging his back on a foam roller every night before bed. And the *Wall Street Journal* ran an article about how the chairs we were using while working at home all day were taking a toll on our backs and necks.[1]

I've always worked from home, so I felt confident that my back pain didn't arise from a problematic desk chair arrangement. I remembered what Anne had always said—that when our backs or necks are tight, we are bracing with anxiety about the future. Hers seemed as accurate a diagnosis as any, and my own new round of back pain pushed me out of denial and into admitting that I was feeling anxious about COVID-19. The pain forced me to pay attention to my fear.

I should note that when I use the word *anxiety* here, I'm referring to the ordinary anxiety most of us experience at some point in our daily lives, not clinical anxiety. I attributed my back pain to ordinary anxiety, but acknowledging that reality wasn't the end of this story. I found myself, like billions of people the world over, scared and anxious and unable to do anything to change the future. Usually, my anxiety gave me energy to work toward a different future than the one I feared. Usually, my anxious energy found what felt like a productive outlet in planning and control. When Penny was little and had four different therapists coming to the house weekly, and I worried about her hitting her developmental milestones, I created a chart with all the possible tactics and exercises we could practice each day. I circled the most important ones so that we could feel successful when we accomplished them. Similarly, when I had a due date looming for a book, I broke down the writing into manageable parts and charted a path that gave me control over the small steps I would need to take to reach that goal. In the course of our ordinary life, I carried a calendar around in my head with details about our schedule for months in advance. It helped me feel calm to know what was coming.

But now, I didn't know what was coming. I had no way to predict the future and even less power to control it. And so I could feel the anxiety, the restless energy that had no place to land. The fear that almost immobilized me because I did not understand how it was possible to move forward into such uncertainty.

For years, I had been in denial about struggling with anxiety. I prided myself on not worrying about our kids' health. I somewhat intentionally did not do a great job of teaching them to wash their hands. I didn't follow all the rules on what I should or shouldn't eat when pregnant. I didn't fear for their safety on playgrounds. I didn't check on them in the middle of the night to make sure they were still breathing. I was able to deny my persistent anxiety because I channeled it into the socially acceptable categories of control and achievement. COVID-19 unmasked my type A planning for what it was—a perpetual and relentless coping mechanism to ward off fear.

Fear—which in our modern era often presents itself as anxiety—keeps us from the healing love of God as much as distraction and shame do. Fear pushes us toward an attempt to control instead of relying and depending on God to care for us, come what may. I look at the story of Jesus with Jairus, and it seems at a certain point that Jesus has failed Jairus. Jairus has humbled himself and sought Jesus out. He has begged for help in front of the crowds and the disciples. He has offered his fears to Jesus, and the word he receives in return is that his daughter has died. It's at this point of utter despondence and helplessness that Jesus calls upon Jairus to resist his fear. Jesus does not tell Jairus what will happen. It's as if Jesus gives Jairus a choice when it comes to healing. Either entrust yourself to my healing love or continue to try to control the outcome. Live in love, or live in fear.

I have often allowed anxiety to energize me when I could be resting in the love of God. That anxiety has fueled relentless activity and striving. My fear of failure as a writer energizes me to scramble to write opinion pieces any time a news story catches my attention, even if it means ignoring our kids or my health or our community. My fear of failure as a mother activates my unwillingness to admit my limits around our household. Instead of acknowledging that I'm never going to enjoy cooking elaborate meals or cultivating a beautiful garden, I push and strive and snap defensive comments at anyone who suggests that the meals are repetitive or the flower beds need attention.

What I've started to realize is that while this energy fuels my productivity, it starves my soul. It activates accomplishment and distances me from love. Anxiety has served me as a fuel for achievement, but it has failed me as a guide to getting well.

The most frequent phrase God says to humans in the Bible is "Do not be afraid."[2] We hear an echo of this command when Jairus's servants approach him to tell him his daughter has died. Jesus turns to Jairus and says, "Do not be afraid; just believe."

My unspoken refrain has been "Do not be afraid. Just control." But the antidote Jesus offers is not control. It is peace by way of presence. In dozens of scriptural moments when God tells humans, "Do not fear," those words are almost always followed by "for I am with you." God's presence—God's loving, saving, restoring, healing presence—is the answer to fear.

Jesus does not assuage the anxiety of his disciples when they want him to move more quickly through his encounters with hurting people. He does not offer Jairus a plan for his daughter's survival. Instead he says, "Do not be afraid. Just believe." Entrust your fear to me. To my love. To my healing power. To my presence, which brings peace.

Six months into the pandemic, it was time for our children to return to school, masked and distanced. One night the week before their return to the classroom, I lay awake for hours. Anxiety dripped into my heart, as if whatever had been keeping it at bay all summer had sprung a leak. Soon I was flooded with doubts and fears—What if the kids don't actually go back? What if I can't meet the deadlines I've agreed to? What if school starts and then they get sent home? What if I fall behind in everything, again?

I made my way back into a restless sleep in the early morning, but when I woke up the fear was still with me. I could feel it in my chest. And yet I also felt that I had a choice. Anxiety, or peace. I could allow the anxiety to energize my day. I could try to take control over the tasks and to-dos and push to conquer the doubts. Or I could relinquish control and plans and productivity. I could receive the day as a gift.

Later that morning, with the choice of what would energize my day still hanging in the balance, I took Penny for her annual visit to the ear doctor. Penny carries a well of painful memories into that office. She's had tubes placed in her ears five or six times. She's had those same tubes extracted with tweezers. Her ear canals are so small that the doctor routinely needs to use a mechanized suction device to clear the wax and debris and fluid out of them. She associates the ear doctor with pain.

So that day, we sat together in the car, waiting for the phone call that would summon us inside. My head was still swimming with worry about the months ahead. Penny took my hand, and she said, "Can we do our prayer breaths, please?" It's a simple practice we had developed over years of routine blood draws and surgeries and thunderstorms and barking dogs and all the other minor and major worries of growing up in her particular body and mind. These "prayer breaths" are also a simple and beautiful and deeply true reminder that anxiety is not the only way to live. We held hands and closed our eyes and breathed in deeply. As we did so, we welcomed God's peace. Then we breathed out, with an audible sigh, and offered our fear to God.

I used to think that releasing anxiety was about letting go. It felt like a defeat, almost, as if I were holding too many toys and books and articles of clothing in my arms and they became too heavy or unwieldy and I just dropped them on the ground and they scattered and broke and made a mess. But the invitation we receive from Jesus is not to let go of our worries but to entrust those worries to God. As Penny and I sat in that gray minivan, we inhaled the promise of God's presence. We handed over our fears with a deep sigh.

In my life, there have been seasons where I handed over those fears in a therapist's office and other times when I have done so in a worship service. I have witnessed the life-changing gift of anti-anxiety medication for multiple friends. God has given us many avenues to get the help we need, including medication and counselors. That day, I was given a reminder of the role of prayer in an ongoing invitation to replace anxiety with peace. Our era has been dubbed the age of anxiety, and neither prayer nor medication nor therapy will change the daily onslaught of reasons to be afraid. But we are invited, every day, to approach God with trust that the Spirit will indeed be with us in the midst of the fear.

When our kids were little, together we memorized one of my favorite Bible passages, Philippians 4:6–7. Here Paul, from behind the bars of a Roman prison, writes, "Do not be anxious about anything, but in everything, by prayer and petition, with thanksgiving, present your requests to God. And the peace of God, which transcends all understanding, will guard your hearts and minds in Christ Jesus." I love the practical wisdom embodied in this passage, wisdom that probably emerged from Paul's own experience of not knowing where his next meal would come from, not knowing whether his message about Jesus would spread or fizzle out, not knowing whether he would live or die. He instructs his fellow new followers of Jesus not to let go of anxiety but to entrust it—"present your requests"—to God. He invites them to "just believe" in the goodness of a God who wants to provide for everything they need. And then he offers them another image that emerges from his direct lived experience as a prisoner. He describes the peace of God as an active force standing guard and protecting their hearts and minds from the anxiety that always threatens to make its way in. Just as physical acts of aggression threaten our bodily well-being, so too does the experience of anxiety threaten the well-being of our souls. Anxiety is a type of violence against our soul, and we can invite the peace of God to stand guard, to protect us and keep us safe.

When we sat in that parking lot, Penny was afraid of a very visceral and tangible reality—that the doctor's visit might cause pain to her ear. I was afraid of more existential threats—that the school year might be routinely disrupted and I might not get to write this book and our kids might feel lonely and I might do a terrible job as a mom and a wife.

Jairus's fear was of a far more dramatic sort. His daughter had died. But for each of us—from Jairus's worst-case scenario to the more mundane worries about the doctor in our minivan—Jesus invites us to know his presence within our fear and to trust him in the midst of that fear. As with distraction and shame, we do not need to overcome the barrier of fear in order to begin a healing journey with Jesus. Healing might only take a moment. More likely, it will take a lifetime, and it will involve not only God's immediate presence but also friends and professionals along the way. But like Jairus, we are called to take the first step along the road with Jesus at our side.

CHAPTER 9

The Barrier of Status

When they came to the home of the synagogue leader, Jesus saw a commotion, with people crying and wailing loudly. He went in and said to them, "Why all this commotion and wailing? The child is not dead but asleep." But they laughed at him.

—MARK 5:38–40

Five of us sat around the table: my husband, my mother, myself, and two medical students who had been assigned to eat dinner at our house. One of the students said, "My parents always wanted more for me—a better education than they had, and a better job, and a higher salary. A better life. So, isn't it hard to have a child with a disability? Don't you want so much more for her?"

These young men were in the midst of a pediatric rotation, and this was their one and only day to learn about children with disabilities. I held three-year-old Penny on my hip as we greeted them at the door in the late afternoon. "Hi," she said, her neck craning to see their faces. Soon enough they were sitting cross-legged on the floor, with Penny pouring tea and offering "tookies."

They spent an hour playing, and once Penny was in bed, we ate together and talked about our family. As the night went on, these prospective doctors grew more and more candid. They told us that earlier in the day they had been asked to consider four different types of disability: spina bifida, cystic fibrosis, Down syndrome, and disfiguring burns. If they were a parent, which one would they want most and least for their child? In ranking those four categories, they had marked Down syndrome as the least desired.

I felt a tightness in my chest as they described that ranking system and their response to it. I felt both the pain of their implicit rejection of our daughter and the pain of how deeply I understood that rejection. The pain of a medical system that even in an attempt to expose discomfort and prejudice reaffirms it. I don't know how I would have answered the same questions in their situation, but I do know that I once walked around with a hierarchy of human beings that implicitly guided my own thinking and behavior. I saw myself as someone near the top of those rankings. And if I was honest, I saw all sorts of other people as those who filled in rungs further down the social ladder.

I constructed an identity around my social position, just like these young men. That identity came from having an able body and access to education. It came from being a white person in America with affluent, married parents. When I applied for a spot at an Ivy League school, I filled out the form that indicated my grandfather had been a student there, too, fifty-five years earlier. When I applied for internships, I relied on the connections of family friends who already worked in Manhattan. When Peter and I wanted to buy our first house, we didn't have trouble securing a loan. It seemed like we built a foundation for our life from responsible decisions and hard work, but in reality, that foundation had been given to us without any work on our part at all. We inherited a set of unearned social advantages that perpetuated themselves. Education begat education. Wealth begat wealth.

But when Penny was diagnosed with an intellectual disability, I could not give her this same inheritance. The fact that she was born into our particular family did set her apart from other, less fortunate, kids—she received healthcare and a mother who could work part-time indefinitely and drive her to doctor's appointments and therapy sessions. She inherited the stability of our household and the "language rich" environment that came with her parents' love for books. She received many unearned social advantages. But she also received—by no effort or fault of her own—the distinctive physical characteristics and cognitive capabilities of a child with a third copy of her twenty-first chromosome. Penny's unexpected and unearned social position brought me face-to-face with the harm of a social ranking system I had never questioned too deeply before.

For the first few years of Penny's life, I thought my job was to advocate for her and for all vulnerable kids who were similarly excluded from access to school or religious communities or social experiences because of disability or race or ethnicity or socioeconomic status. I pushed for inclusion in swim lessons and dance class. I became more progressive in my view toward healthcare policy. I voted for the politicians who advocated for universal preschool because I now believed every kid deserves access to learning during those early years of brain development. I wrote about the harm inherent in the words *retarded* and *abnormal*. I pointed out the problems with a medicalized view of humanity.

I advocated fiercely for Penny, for other kids with disabilities, and for other vulnerable kids more generally. I saw inclusion as the goal. I wanted to knock down the social barriers to a world that excluded Penny but welcomed me. I wanted to invite her in. I worked to give her, and other kids like her, a hand up the ladder, so to speak.

I saw the way this social hierarchy harmed Penny and yet I failed to see the way that same hierarchy was harming me. As I spent more time with Penny and more time interacting with other people with disabilities, I began to recognize that the harm of social exclusion was mirrored by the harm of social isolation. I lived in a bubble of homogeneity that isolated me from the beauty, goodness, and diversity of humanity. I failed to understand the value of the people outside my own social world, and in so doing, I failed to understand the fullness of our shared humanity. Just like those young men at our kitchen table.

When they told us about the ranking they had been asked to do in class, and when they admitted that Down syndrome was at the bottom of their list, they did so because being in our home had changed their understanding of what it means to live with Down syndrome. When they left, they told us they were grateful for the evening not so much because it influenced their career as doctors, but because it had changed them as individuals. They had been humbled by the opportunity to come to value another human being, in this case a human being with Down syndrome. One of them flushed red as he said, "I would love to have a family just like this."

I could envision Jesus at our kitchen table telling those students that for all their hard work and good grades and accolades, they weren't any more important than this little girl with glasses, a speech delay, and a hearing loss. I could envision Jesus explaining that they each had something of equal worth to contribute to God's work in this world. The kingdom of heaven had come among us, for just a moment, when those students saw Penny as a gift, as a beloved child. A little act of repair happened when we bridged that dividing line between patient and doctor, intellectually astute and intellectually disabled, between those admired and esteemed by our society and those deemed "abnormal" and undesirable.

From what the Gospels tell us, the religious leaders were the least likely people to receive Jesus' message. They were also the least likely to experience Jesus' healing. In their culture, more so than ours, religious leadership was a hallmark of social standing, kind of like being a CEO of a company or the mayor of a town. These respectable, powerful, relatively wealthy and educated people were the most likely to ignore, avoid, or reject Jesus—unless, like Jairus, something made them aware of their need for everything Jesus had to offer.

We can guess that Jairus was earnest and good and hardworking. He was a man with a reputation to preserve. He had social status as a religious leader. For him to kneel, publicly, at the feet of a controversial, poor, renegade preacher would not help his standing in the community. But he was desperate. His daughter was dying. Love pushed Jairus through the barrier of social status. Love gave him access to Jesus. Love gave him access to healing.

Most of us want to rely on our own sense of self-sufficiency and independence rather than turn to Jesus for help. For me, for Jairus, the trappings of status erect a barrier to admitting our need. Respectability, power, wealth, esteem. All of them can keep us from understanding our need for healing. Jesus himself says, "It is easier for a camel to go through the eye of a needle than for someone who is rich to enter the kingdom of

God" (Mark 10:25). Social status erects a spiritual wall within our souls.

I can't shake the thought that Jesus wanted Jairus to encounter the bleeding woman on his way home to his dying daughter. Not only to see Jesus' love and care for this outcast woman. Not only to witness how Jesus disregards social divisions and dismisses categories of exclusion. But also for Jairus to see his own connection to a woman he would have considered beneath him. To see their common humanity. Their common vulnerability and desperate need. Their common belovedness.

I wonder whether Jairus stood on the sidelines and watched as Jesus cured this woman of her bleeding, called her *Daughter*, commended her for her faith, and sent her out in peace. I wonder whether Jairus witnessed something that called to his own humanity, that bridged his society's dividing lines, that opened up new possibilities for healing. I wonder whether Jesus cared not only about healing Jairus's daughter of her illness but also about healing Jairus himself of the invisible wounds that come from standing atop a social hierarchy and looking down on those below.

Over the course of these past fifteen years of starting to unlearn the Western value system that says my social status gives me worth, I've started to see the harm done to all of us through these social hierarchies. I've begun to understand how unearned social advantages lead to unjust social divisions. I've also begun to see how those divisions erect barriers to healing. Jesus offers healing to everyone, yet he also recognizes that whole groups of people don't understand their own need for that healing, and unless they can recognize that need, the barriers to healing will remain in place.

The tragic irony behind so many of our social divisions becomes clear when we see the ways they harm everyone—including those who seem to have materially bene-fited from them. Decades ago, reflecting on his own position as a white southerner, Wendell Berry wrote, "If white people have suffered less obviously from racism than black people, they have nevertheless suffered greatly; the cost has been greater perhaps than we can yet know . . . the wound is there, and it is a profound disorder, as great a damage in his mind as it is in his society."[1] Berry writes about the distortions that come to us as individuals and as a society when we fail to recognize and receive one another in our common and full humanity.

More recently, in *The Sum of Us: What Racism Costs Every-one and How We Can Prosper Together*, Heather McGhee has argued that structural racism within the United States has adversely affected everyone economically, socially, and as a civic society. To cite but one of her multitude of examples, she explains how the integration of public pools led many commu-nities to shut their pools down altogether. Neither Black nor white children could swim. "A once-public resource became a luxury amenity, and entire communities lost out," she writes.[2] Because of the barrier of social status, everyone lost. On both the level of our abstract humanity and the level of our prag-matic decisions around creating safe communities, our refusal to acknowledge and receive one another across social dividing lines harms us all. To repair the harm of individual and struc-tural racism and other unjust social divisions, we will all need to receive healing.

A strange moment is recorded in all three synoptic gospels when Jesus says, "It is not the healthy who need a doctor, but the sick" (see Matthew 9:12; Mark 2:17; Luke 5:31). At first glance, Jesus seems to imply that people with high social status and religious power don't need him. And since those people aren't needy, he approaches the people who are—the sick and disabled and outcast. The weird thing about this comment is that Jesus is at a dinner party when he says it. He is not standing in the middle of a doctor's office. No one around him appears to be sick. He has not arrived at the dinner party straight from a scene of miraculous healing. He simply sits down at the table and says, "It is not the healthy who need a doctor, but the sick."

Up until this moment, Jesus has been doing all sorts of things to announce the presence of God's anointed one, the Messiah. He has been healing people, and teaching in the synagogues, and generally gaining approval for his righteousness. But now he is celebrating among known tax collectors and "sinners" (see Mark 2:15).[3] The religious authorities of his time and place do not approve.[4]

This moment offers yet another window into the reality that, for Jesus, healing goes deeper than physical transformation. For Jesus, healing is about restoring the whole person. Healing is about the body and the mind and the spirit, which means that healing is about physical care, social connection, and spiritual restoration. Only the ones who know their "sickness," who recognize their need for healing, will approach the doctor and receive the doctor's care. These include the sinners and tax collectors at the dinner party, who stand in contrast to most of the religious leaders who reject Jesus. The poor and outcast ones, like the bleeding woman. The rich and powerful who have been humbled, like Jairus.

In placing the stories of Jairus and the bleeding woman side by side, Mark has invited us to see not only the comparisons and contrasts inherent within them, but also the way the healings are interrelated. Jesus' healing is about the individual in the context of a community and a society. The individual barriers to healing—distraction, shame, fear—are compounded by the communal barriers to healing, the social hierarchies that lead to exclusion, isolation, and injustice.

I mentioned earlier that Matthew links Jesus' name with his healing/saving work. Again, English Bibles record the angel of the Lord appearing to Joseph and telling him, "You are to give him the name Jesus, because he will save his people from their sins" (Matthew 1:21). We could also read these words as "He will heal his people from their sins." I grew up thinking of "sins" as vices. Things like stealing, cheating, lying, gossip. Choices we made as individuals that went against God's instructions for how we should behave. And I thought that verses that seemed to conflate sin and sickness made sense. If you break God's law, you may well experience pain and suffering. Jesus is the Great Physician who heals us of our sin, whether that's the sin of debauchery or the sin of pride.

It can seem simplistic: sin and sickness go together. The problem with putting sin and healing in the same sentence is that linking sin to brokenness or suffering can lead us to cast judgment on those experiencing pain and illness. We easily assign blame to the sufferer and absolve everyone else from responsibility. The disciples and the religious leaders of Jesus' time assumed that pain and disability came because of bad behavior, and so do many of us today. We blame people with type 2 diabetes for overeating, lung cancer patients for smoking, and chronic migraine sufferers for a failure to relax. And just like the disciples, when we can't find a direct cause for illness here and now, we look to the parents. Psychologists in the 1950s attributed autism to emotionally "frozen" mothers. In recent years, parents have been blamed for everything from childhood obesity to anxiety.

We do sometimes experience bodily pain and illness because of sinful choices. There is a relationship between sin and suffering. It's just a far more complicated truth than any formulaic assignment of blame allows. I think of all the kids growing up with asthma in American cities today. Surely they—and their parents—are not to blame for the poor air quality in their neighborhoods that contributes to a life-threatening lung disease. Or the kids in Flint, Michigan, who suffered physical and intellectual harm because of lead in their water. In both cases, we can name the sin of a wealthy society that fails to care enough about the vulnerable lives of children to do whatever it takes to provide clean air and water to all its members. But those individuals, those communities, are not at fault. They bear the sickness without bearing the sin. Sin's relationship to our bodies is complex, and our guilt is often collective rather than personal. The collective sin of injustice causes harm on a collective level.

Jesus does not dismiss the role of sin in suffering. He tells various people, after they have received healing, to "sin no more" (see John 5:14; 8:11). He forgives a paralyzed man before helping him walk again. But he also repudiates the simplistic logic that leads people to think catastrophes harm only sinners who deserved their fate. Jesus assumes all people are sinners. He calls all people to repentance. If anything, Jesus commends rather than condemns sinners because they are more likely to recognize their need for grace.

The communal healing God wants for us can happen only when we are able to admit our common need for God and receive one another across the lines of social division. People like Jairus, like me, often live in a social world cut off from the beauty, diversity, and goodness of the expanse of humanity— like the doctors who had never interacted with a child with an intellectual disability and found themselves broadened and enriched by having a tea party with her.

I have spent much of my life isolated from people of color, people with disabilities, people who have different educations and skills and beliefs and backgrounds from me. Which means not only that I have participated in unjust systems and structures that perpetuate the advantages I receive within our society, but also that I have missed out on the fuller, richer, deeper understanding of humanity available to me through encounters with a diverse range of people.

Social status builds a barrier that keeps us from admitting our need for the healing love of God. Social hierarchies keep us from giving and receiving love and care across social boundaries and with one another. These hierarchies perpetuate injustice, and we become complicit in that injustice. If there's anything we've seen in contemporary society that resonates with the world of Jesus, it's that social hierarchies are still in place and that exclusion, isolation, and injustice continue to keep us from healing.

Jairus is a man who knows his own need for Jesus. On the one hand, he is healthy—he has the status and power and wealth and morality and religious stability that he needs in order to take care of his household. And then his daughter's illness breaks through and shows him his vulnerability, his "sickness," his need for Jesus. Here, Jairus is unusual. Over and over throughout the Gospels, Jesus rebukes the religious leaders both because they fail to see their own need and because they fail to see those in need all around them. They fail to care for the ones in prison, the sick, the hungry, the homeless. They fail to rescue the lost sheep, the ones who have wandered away or who have been harmed by no fault of their own.[5]

People like Jairus run the risk of not knowing their own need for healing, but they also run the risk of judging and distancing themselves from others who are in obvious need. They can begin to believe that their own status is a sign of health, of God's favor upon them, when in fact their status is an invitation to connect with and offer care for other needy people.

The barriers of distraction, shame, and anxiety seem formidable enough. Adding the barrier of status and injustice to the mix makes it seem all the more impossible for any of us to receive or participate in the healing that God wants us to experience. But I look back to the love that prompted Jairus to admit his own need and fall at Jesus' feet. I think back to those students who encountered a real little girl and saw her humanity. I think back to myself, where love for a child broke through the years of assumptions and gave me a different understanding of what it means to live a full life. And once again, I return to hope that healing depends not on my own ability to fix problems or become perfect, but rather on Jesus' willingness to come to us in our weakness, need, and divisions and make us well.

PART III

Participation in Healing

CHAPTER 10

Bodily Healing

Daughter, your faith has healed you.

—MARK 5:34

When I was a freshman in college, I was sick enough that I commuted home every weekend of the second semester. After a stint in the emergency room that December, everyone agreed I wasn't up for the intensity of college life. But I refused to withdraw altogether, so I came up with a plan whereby I took three classes so I could arrive at school on Monday morning and come home Thursday evening in time for a Friday session with a therapist and a few days of rest.

On those weekends, I always changed trains in Manhattan. From Penn Station, I took the subway up to Grand Central, where I bought a ticket for Riverside, Connecticut, and boarded a Metro-North car. But one night, as I exited the escalator in Penn Station and headed toward the subway, a man asked if I wanted a five-dollar cab ride, and I said yes. He walked me to a line of taxis, took my five dollars, opened the door for me, and sent me on my way. Even as I was handing him the money, I knew it was a scam. I would be paying the cab driver a separate fare. My face burned in the back seat.

The next day, I told the therapist about the man who stole the five dollars. She asked me how I felt.

I shrugged. "Embarrassed. Mad at myself for not realizing sooner what was happening."

"How about toward him? Were you angry at him?"

I stared at her, trying to imagine what that would feel like. "No," I said. "I don't get angry."

I thought I was telling the truth.

I learned early on, from both my family and my larger social context, that the most acceptable way to be in the world was "fine." Not shouting in rage or joy. Not crying in ecstasy or sorrow. Expressing myself through measured words and emotions. I learned that feelings were out of control. They didn't win arguments. They didn't belong in essays or spread-sheets. Feelings didn't get good grades or win awards. They were unpredictable, unreliable. By the time I was sitting in that therapist's office, I didn't know what it was like to feel anger. I didn't know what it was like to feel much of anything at all.

It took years for me to realize that I did have emotions, I just didn't feel them in the ways I expected. It took years for me to understand that my body itself was carrying messages of emotional pain and spiritual need. It took years for me to learn how to begin to connect my body to my mind and my spirit. When I look at the healing stories in the Gospels, it becomes clear that healing begins when we come to Jesus in our bodies, with our neediness and helplessness and our far-from-perfect faith and our fears and distractions and bumbling efforts. The bleeding woman reaches out her hand. Jairus falls at Jesus' feet.

People like me, who often deny the body's natural limits, who ignore pain and discomfort, who think about things instead of feeling them, need to learn how to come to God in our bodies.

As a young woman, I could see that my sickness in high school and college had as much to do with my mind and spirit as my body. But I didn't make those same connections in my adult life until that moment I sat down with Anne. I labored with three babies, recovered from an appendectomy, went to bed with scarlet fever, and suffered through countless other minor illnesses and pains—all without connecting my bodily distress to anything else, all without asking God to be involved. But when I started to really dig into the dozens of stories of Jesus healing people, I began to believe that God cares about how we experience our bodies. God invites us to bring our heartbreaks and shame and fear. God also invites us to bring our aching backs and sniffling noses, our cancer diagnoses and autoimmune diseases, our anxiety and depression. Though healing is far more than bodily cures, and it doesn't always eliminate pain or disease, it always includes coming to God in our bodies.

Mark records that as soon as the woman touches Jesus' cloak, Jesus feels power "go out" from him. Just as suddenly, and simultaneously, Mark writes, "her bleeding stopped" (Mark 5:29). It's pretty simple. She reaches out. Jesus' power flows. Her body and spirit respond. It seems clear: Jesus' power heals her.

But Jesus talks about this encounter differently. He says to this woman, "Your faith has healed you."

Wait. What?

What does her faith have to do with anything? Sure, she reached out her hand, but it was his power that made the difference. Wasn't it?

And this isn't the only story in the Gospels where Jesus uses these words to commend a person who has been healed. He gives exactly the same affirmation to the sinful woman anointing his feet with her tears. He repeats these words to a leper, and yet again to a blind man named Bartimaeus after he receives his sight (see Luke 7:36–50; 17:11–19; Mark 10:46–52). As I've noted before, these words get translated differently in our Bibles depending on their different contexts: Your faith has *healed* you. Your faith has *saved* you. But in Greek the statements are exactly the same. In some mysterious way, this woman has participated in her own healing.

Elsewhere, Jesus gives people direct instructions for participating in their own healing. "Pick up your mat and walk," he tells a paralyzed man. "Go wash yourself," he says to a man born blind. "Stretch out your hand," he commands a man with a withered hand (see John 5:1–18; 9:1–12; Mark 3:1–6). These men and women come to Jesus in their bodies, asking for help from a place of desperate need. And, according to Jesus, somehow these men and women also play a part in their own miraculous transformation. They participate in their own healing.

For Jesus, healing is holistic, connecting body, mind, and spirit. Healing is personal, reconnecting our lives to the love of God. Healing is humbling, dependent on our acknowledgment of need and helplessness. But healing is also participatory. Without taking away from the power of his own presence, Jesus nevertheless emphatically states that this healing relies on our participation within it.

The idea that humans participate in God's saving, healing work can set off theological alarm bells. One central concept within Christianity is the unmerited forgiveness offered to us through Jesus' death and the unmerited salvation, wholeness,

restoration, and healing offered to us through his ongoing resurrection life. Healing is not an achievement any more than
salvation is an achievement. It is all an act of grace, a free gift
freely given.

But to extend this analogy a bit, a gift is experienced only
when the recipient opens it and employs it for its purpose.
Jesus has done the work of healing. The power has gone out
from him to the woman who has exhausted all other options.
It would be easy to conclude that Jesus is the one, the only
one, who deserves commendation in this transaction. But the
bleeding woman—this woman whom Jesus names *Daughter*—is not a passive or unwitting recipient of God's love and
grace. She is an active participant in her own healing, in her
own restoration to her community, and in her own relationship with God.

This woman's faith was at best incomplete. She comes to
Jesus trembling in fear, which implies she has a limited understanding of Jesus' love and compassion. Her faith may even
have been built on superstition, thinking all she needs is to
touch his cloak, as if it were a magical talisman. She doesn't
come looking for an encounter with Jesus. She simply wants
whatever miracle might flow from this holy man. But Jesus
doesn't critique or evaluate her faith. He doesn't parse the dis-
tinctions between his healing power and her actions. Rather,
he uses this moment to draw attention to her, to honor her.
Like a proud parent whose toddler has taken one wobbly step.

For those of us who have so far lived in bodies without
chronic pain or illness or disability, we nevertheless experience
bodily need and sensation daily. We experience fatigue and
hunger, pulled muscles and sniffly noses. We come to the world
in a variety of shapes and sizes with different abilities and limits on what we are able to do with our limbs and torsos and

eyes and ears. We all experience delight in our bodies—a thrill of excitement when we see someone we love, the feeling of warmth and comfort upon tasting a delicious meal. We also all experience physical pain. Pain reminds me that I live in a body, that my body matters, that my mind and spirit depend on my body every moment of every day. Pain and illness and even discomfort often serve as a starting place for turning to Jesus. As I began to understand the connection between mind, body, and spirit that was both present in the stories about Jesus and necessary for my own healing today, I realized how much I wanted to learn how to connect my body, mind, and spirit.

I wondered what practices we can employ today to make these connections between the physical, emotional, and spiritual aspects of our being. How can we, too, participate in healing?

For me, participation often begins by noticing when pain comes to my body. I now pay attention to a restless night of sleep, an aching back, a burning sensation in my shoulder, a headache, a runny nose, a stomachache. And I try to notice any emotions that accompany it—shame, fear, anger, hurt, sadness. But because I am so trained in repressing emotions, I often can't come up with anything. So then I consider what was going on in my life around the time the pain started. I remember that tense conversation with Peter, that regrettable moment with one of our kids, that sharply worded email. I notice that my thoughts had wandered to my to-do list, and I start to wonder whether that tightness in my neck comes from worry about having too much to accomplish.

Noticing the pain and wondering whether it connects to something going on in my soul is a first step. The next step is to bring that pain to Jesus for healing. As I've already noted in these pages, I don't think prayer is the only way to handle physical pain. I gladly take medication for pain, and many doctors who acknowledge the emotional roots of much of our pain will begin with prescribing medication as a way to open up space for deeper healing. I've learned that I am most likely to see the pain go away permanently if I enter into the deeper interior work. I also very much believe in the healing power of connecting with other humans in our pain—whether through support groups or therapy or spiritual direction or friendship. Healing happens when I begin to ask God's Spirit to help me understand not only the physical pain but the hurts and fears and shame within my soul. Healing happens when I bring prayer into my body and allow the Spirit to connect my disparate parts and connect me to other people.

The Bible is filled with references to how our bodies feel when we are anxious or depressed or distant from God. The psalmists describe their bones aching, their mouths parched and dry, their backs weighed down. Paul mentions a thorn in his side that is never removed. His words can be taken metaphorically, but it is also likely that Paul carried pain in his body all the time. Some of these passages lead to prayers that alleviate pain. Others, as in Paul's experience, do not. In either case, the pain serves as an invitation to come to God in our bodies, and the specific pain we are experiencing can become a guide to prayer.

So when my shoulders are aching with tension, I pray with the reminder that Jesus' yoke is easy and his burden is light. When my chest is tight with anxiety, I pray that the Spirit would "guard my heart" with the "peace that passes all understanding." When my Achilles stings, I pray that I would be "rooted and grounded in God's love."[1] Sometimes I even take the body part that is hurting and type it into a Bible search engine to see what passages come up. Or I ask God to bring a specific story or passage to mind, or a simple prayer that speaks truth to my soul. Even when the pain or discomfort remains, bringing that pain, those feelings, the memories and thoughts to God helps awaken my spirit to needs that go beyond physical pain.

There is nothing magical about these prayers. I am not healing myself. I am reaching out to the Lord, the God who created me as a person with this body, this mind, and this spirit. Like the woman in the crowd, I am reaching out for healing.

But what about pain that doesn't go away? What about bodies that age? What about terminal illness? It all still offers an invitation to come to Jesus with our whole selves, whether to rage or to grieve or even to give thanks for the good we can cling to in the midst of the suffering.

The Christian tradition includes many other ways to bring prayer to the body and to involve the body in prayer and in the work of reconnection. Pastor Mindy Roll writes about learning how to connect to her body in prayer. For her, this didn't happen through noticing pain. The process began with "checking in" with her body, scanning from head to toe and everything in between. She first asked where her attention lingered. She then "listened" to any emotion associated with that place, and waited for a story that might emerge from it. She describes practicing this type of prayer after the birth of her first child, and how she became "overwhelmed by the sense that God was offering God's own nurture and tenderness in the places where my tired body had nurtured life."[2]

In her book *An Altar in the World*, priest and professor Barbara Brown Taylor writes about another way to bring prayer to our bodies: "I think it is important to pray naked in front of a full-length mirror sometimes, especially when you are full of loathing for your body." She encourages us to recognize that our bodies are "our soul's address." We live as full selves within these particular bodies—with illness and pain, with parts we love and parts we would rather keep covered. And bringing our whole and real bodies to God in prayer can change us. Taylor continues, "When I do this, I generally decide that it is time to do a better job of wearing my skin with gratitude instead of loathing. No matter what I think of my body, I can still offer it to God to go on being useful to the world."[3]

Other church traditions have connected the body to the mind, emotion, and spirit in practices like kneeling in confession or raising hands in praise, using the body to express the posture of the heart. Some incorporate dance in worship as yet another way to connect the body and the spirit. And although we don't always think of it as making a connection between the physical and the spiritual, the act of singing is yet another longstanding Christian tradition that can bring prayer into our bodies and bring our bodies into prayer.

Through the centuries, some Christians have also used labyrinths as a method of embodied prayer. Labyrinths contain the same general design from place to place. There are no dead ends, and no wrong turns. To walk a labyrinth is always an invitation to follow a circuitous path to the center. There is only one way in, and only one way out. And that winding path serves as a physical way to envision a season of life or even life as a whole. Walking a labyrinth offers an embodied reminder that while we often want our life's path to be like a straight line to a clear destination, it takes lots of twists and turns, and we often feel as though we are headed in entirely the wrong direction. This curving reality repeats itself again and again. The journey through life is like a circle that nevertheless has an ultimate direction and destination. It is not endless repetition, but guided wandering—with lots of doubling back and falling away from the center and returning, again and again.

I suspect that those of us who follow Jesus also have a lot to learn from spiritual traditions outside of Christianity about practices of connecting the body to the mind and the spirit. But the resources available within Christianity alone, starting with people in the Bible who come to God in their bodies and continuing throughout the history of the church, provide us with multiple ways to signal our desire to welcome God's healing work into our lives.

The bleeding woman reaches out. Jairus falls at Jesus' feet. For us, participation in healing begins with bringing our real pain, our real needs, our real bodies—to Jesus. It continues as we receive his healing touch and allow him to connect our bodies, minds, and spirits and begin to make us well.

CHAPTER 11

Spiritual Healing

Daughter, your faith has healed you.

—MARK 5:34

As we were turning the corner from the school year to the summer a while back, I knew I would be tempted to drink wine every night of the week, as if I were on vacation for three months straight. I also knew that wasn't a good idea. The evenings when friends came to town, or when we had a long dinner followed by an hour around the firepit with extended family weren't my concern. I wanted a plan for the nights when Peter was working and I was at home and the kids didn't need me to drive them to activities all over the county and I didn't really have anything I needed to do and so instead of facing my fear of not being productive I would drink some rosé.

I asked Anne if she could suggest a physical practice that would help me address this potentially destructive habit. She suggested starting my day by setting a timer for seven minutes and breathing slowly, inhaling peace and exhaling anxiety.[1] Over the course of that summer, I began to modify those instructions. Sometimes I imagined the peace of God filling my body and soul on the inhale. And I imagined entrusting all my worries and fears to Jesus on the exhale. On other days, I used this breath pattern, this time of prayer, to sink into God's love. I inhaled and imagined the love of God filling my being. I exhaled and imagined that same love surrounding me, protecting me, holding me close and safe.

When the afternoon came, and I thought about how I wanted to end the day with wine, my morning practice interrupted my thoughts. I took a few breaths, reminding my body that there was another way to receive peace and rest. Over time, my drinking habits changed. Those seven minutes gave me a way to practice receiving the love of God. They gave me a taste of the way love can heal us.

When Jesus encounters the bleeding woman, he responds with love. That love is made manifest in his public affirmation of her status before God: *Daughter*. He also reminds us what love looks like when he commends her participation in her own healing. *Your faith has healed you.*

Love welcomes, but it doesn't coerce. Love beckons, but it doesn't control. Love shares. Love, by its nature, is relational. It invites our response. It invites our participation. Love is humble, and Jesus' humility is on display here. Jesus never seeks out attention for his miraculous deeds. He turns the spotlight to the person in need. He elevates the other person.

God's own humility is on display throughout the Bible as God welcomes us—we who are God's beloved and bumbling creation—into the work of redemption. God's love welcomes our involvement in understanding our own need for healing and reaching out to touch the hem of his garment as he passes our way.

This woman follows a sequence that is similiar to other encounters with Jesus throughout the Gospels. She acknowledges her own need. She reaches out for help. And she receives the healing love of Jesus. Over two thousand years later, we are invited to follow this pattern in order to participate in our own healing. We too can acknowledge our need, reach out for help, and receive Jesus' healing love.

Jairus also acknowledges need, reaches out for help, and receives Jesus' love. In front of people who know him as powerful and strong, Jairus admits his weakness, his helplessness. He says, "My little daughter is dying. Please come and put your hands on her so that she will be healed and live" (Mark 5:23). It's an intimate request, one that recognizes Jesus' compassion, the way Jesus is known to care for people as individuals. It's also a very specific request. Jairus names his desire. He wants life for his daughter. In the midst of the fear of losing her, he holds on to enough hope that he speaks aloud the fullness of what he envisions for her future. And Jesus comes with him.

If we are to follow the path of healing, we must not only acknowledge our needs, but also express our desires. Both Jairus and the bleeding woman recognize their neediness, and they reach out to Jesus to bring the healing love of God to their situations.

This second step in healing is to ask for help, which is to say, to open ourselves up to the possibility of healing that arrives from an external source. Asking God for help is not a glitzy production. Jairus uses the words *Please come*. The woman reaches out her hand without even speaking. His words and her gesture are simple and sincere. They emerge out of humility. Jairus and the woman know their need. They know they cannot heal themselves. And they know that Jesus offers hope in the midst of that helplessness.

For those of us who find ourselves aware of our need for healing—healing from physical pain, healing in relationships, healing in our divided society—we too can ask God for help in simple terms, without fanfare or impressive theological knowledge or wellsprings of faith. Neither Jairus nor the bleeding woman has absolute trust in Jesus. They come, trembling. They come with doubts. And Jesus responds.

I glimpsed the power of earnestly asking God for help years ago when Grand Penny, Peter's mom, spent a weekend with us. We were newly married, in our mid-twenties. She was a single woman who had been sad and lonely for a long time. We had been talking all weekend about that sadness and loneliness, and finally she asked, "Will you pray with me?"

I remember her prayer because it was so brief and honest. She said, "Lord, help me."

It sounds reductionistic to say that prayer was all it took, and yet her life changed in that moment. She connected to God in a new way, with a new desire to read the Bible and talk to God personally. We didn't know that cancer cells were already multiplying in her liver, that four months later she would receive her diagnosis, that less than a year after that she would experience profound healing in her relationship to herself, to God, and to others, and that we would need to say goodbye. All we knew was that she knew her own neediness and asked Jesus to respond to her. That simple prayer indicated her willingness to receive whatever love God wanted to pour into her life. *Daughter*, I can imagine Jesus saying to her, *your faith has made you well.*

We take the first steps toward participating in God's healing activity in our own lives when we acknowledge our needs and ask for help. When we do so, it is as if we open a vessel inside our souls, a place of receptivity. From that position, we can receive the healing love of God. Jesus' words in Matthew 11:28 offer us an image of what it looks like to bring our needs to God and receive from God in return: "Come to me, all you who are weary and burdened, and I will give you rest."

The love of God takes many forms. It can come by way of individual experiences. It can also come by way of a neighbor who brings a meal or offers a ride. It can come through a doctor's care or a therapist's gentle question. It can come through a song on the radio, a passage of scripture, a walk in the woods. God comes to us—by God's Spirit—in a multitude of ways when we ask for help. But underneath everything from hospitals to baked chickens, miracles to dreams and visions, is God's love.

Once I began to see this simple pattern of acknowledging need, asking for help, and receiving love, I began to wonder how I could participate in this type of healing here and now. I learned how to bring prayer to my body when I had acute pain or illness, and I also began to wonder what practices I could put in place to receive God's love on a daily basis. My thoughts and prayers rested on a passage from Ephesians where Paul prays that his readers would be "rooted and established in love" (3:17). That image of sinking roots down into love—as if love was the soil and my life was a sapling stretching toward the light—gave me a framework for how I could actively participate in healing by connecting to God's love.

Receiving God's love like a tree receives water comes up throughout the Bible. Jesus compares humans to seeds that, when established in good soil, will grow and flourish (Mark 4:13–20). Elsewhere, when Jesus talks about how his disciples can stay connected to him, he compares himself to a vine, and he exhorts his followers to "remain in his love" like a branch remains in a vine, in order to live (see John 15:9). And again, Paul picks up on this imagery when he exhorts his readers to be "rooted and established" in the love of God and "rooted" in Christ (see Ephesians 3:17; Colossians 2:6–7).

All these passages return to the idea that we rely on love and strength from outside ourselves in order to grow and flourish. A tree at a nursery, with roots bundled up or dangling in midair, is a tree destined for death, unless someone purchases it and transplants it. Like trees, we need to be planted and connected to soil and water in order to thrive. We need to get in touch with the God who exists outside of us, the Love that creates and forms and reforms us. In asking for help, we are opening ourselves up to the love of God, like a tree opens itself up to nourishment. We are longing for healing that comes from the outside in. And even before any healing comes, when we ask for help, we are expressing hope, like a tree stretching out its roots in soil for the first time, ready to grow.

Peter Wohlleben, a forester from Germany, wrote a bestselling book called *The Hidden Life of Trees* in which he explains the role that roots play in sustaining the life of a tree. According to Wohlleben, "The root is a more decisive factor than what is growing above ground."[2] He explains the basics: roots nourish, anchor, and connect. Roots draw the nutrients of the soil into the tree so that it can grow and bear fruit. Similarly, as we learn how to root ourselves in the love of God, we receive nourishment from that love. Roots expand wider than their respective tree is tall, so that even when powerful wind lashes their branches, the roots hold the trees in the ground. When we face the inevitable storms that will come our way, God's love will hold us in place even when we feel as though we might topple over.

Roots also connect to the roots of other trees. Not only do these roots overlap in such a way that they hold one another up, strengthening them all in the face of a storm, but they also share nourishment with one another. If one tree is growing in rocky soil and another is nearby in loamy soil and those trees' roots connect, they can share resources and even grow at the same rate. Yes, God's love anchors us and nourishes us, but as God's people connect to one another, we also begin to anchor and nourish one another.

Jesus embodies that same love when he calls the woman *Daughter* and when he takes Jairus's little girl by the hand and raises her to life. For us to join the bleeding woman and Jairus in an experience of healing, we need to acknowledge our need, ask Jesus for help, and then open ourselves up to the healing power of his love, just as they did.

God's love comes up in hundreds of places throughout the Bible. This love is the undercurrent of the whole story told in Jewish and Christian Scripture, and there are a few passages where the writers dwell explicitly on the nature of that love. God promises to show love "to a thousand generations" (Exodus 20:6). The most quoted passage in the Hebrew Bible is from Exodus 34 in which the writers declare that God is "compassionate and gracious, abounding in love and faithfulness."[3] These words provide us with a guide into the heart of God. When I take the time to contemplate the simple but unexpected statements about love found in the New Testament—*Love is patient. Love is kind. Love keeps no record of wrongs . . . God is love. Whoever lives in love lives in God, and God in them . . . As the Father has loved me, so have I loved you. Now remain in my love* (see 1 Corinthians 13:4–5; 1 John 4:16b; John 15:9)—I begin to recognize how different God's way of being is from my own. I've spent years considering what it might mean to root myself in the love of Christ, to reach out in meager faith for the hem of his garment, to participate in the healing work that God wants to do in my life. Teachers from throughout the ages and wise leaders here and now have all helped me develop practices that enable those roots to sink down deep into the soil of God's love.

Jesus teaches that the words found within the Bible provide us with much of what we need to grow in faith. From beginning to end, there are hundreds of passages about the love of God, and using those passages as a guide to prayer helps me put my trust in that love. Reading those passages slowly and with time to reflect helps me see my own need and ask God for help in it.

Similarly, I use prayer to imagine myself receiving Jesus' love. I imagine myself as the woman in Mark 5, trembling with fear and then hearing the word *Daughter*. I imagine myself as the blind man crying out for Jesus' healing and then following him along the way. I imagine Jesus looking upon me with love, care, and compassion, just as he looks at the people who came to him when he walked the earth.

The spiritual leaders I most admire all talk or write about spending time in contemplative prayer to rest in the love of God. The instructions seem simple enough. They sit, daily, in the presence of God's love. I'm still grappling with what that means. My thoughts distract me within seconds whenever I try to settle into God's presence. I find myself remembering things like needing new underwear and running out of limes and worrying that no one will like my Instagram post today. And then I remember to return to prayer. To return to the love of God. And then I think about the grocery list again.

I've read whole books about contemplative prayer. I've listened to podcasts dedicated to the topic. It still feels pretty vague to me. Do these people really take twenty minutes twice a day to sit in God's presence with only one word or phrase on repeat, bringing themselves back again and again to the ephemeral reality of love? Do they actually feel God's love in that time? Maybe someday I will be like them and this will "work" and make sense to me. For now, I am learning to participate in God's healing, learning to sink my roots into the soil of God's love, through a variety of different types of prayer, including my own meager attempts to rest in God's presence.

I do sometimes sit cross-legged in a comfortable armchair, my tea steaming at my side. I take a sip, close my eyes, and follow the way of the contemplatives and repeat one word or phrase. There are days when I just use the word *love*, or the phrase *God is love*, or the invitation *Abide in love*. I am still working through years of lies that I have believed about myself: "You can't stop working or you'll stop receiving love. You should have done better. You aren't enough." Thankfully, God's love can drown out those lies, and gently, like warm water pouring over my head and running down my shoulders and torso and washing me clean, God's love can tenderly heal my soul from the harm those lies have caused. Heal my soul with the truth of the love that is the most true thing of all.

Jairus and the bleeding woman, for all we know, had not spent hours in silent contemplation when they approached Jesus. They simply knew their need and were both humble and courageous enough to ask for help. Prayer—whether that looks like hours of contemplation or a moment of expressing heartfelt need—is one way we sink our roots into the soil of God's love. Another way to receive God's love comes not through a solitary spiritual exercise but rather through interaction with other people. We can receive the love of God by letting other people love us. Jesus returned people to their communities with the intention that their healing would continue in and among one another. When we give and receive love, we reflect on and respond to God's love within God's people. Especially for people who do a lot of loving and serving others—for those of us who show up with the baked chicken as soon as the neighbor has a baby or the friend gets sick—we might need to allow other people to love us in order to recognize that God's love is for us too.

I have also found that imagining God's love for other people helps me imagine it for myself. A few years ago, I had the honor of offering the bread and wine during communion at my grandmother's funeral. Before then, when I took communion, I would return to my seat and close my eyes and pray. But after the experience of verbalizing the truth—*This is Christ's body, broken for you . . . This is the cup of salvation*—I started to keep my eyes open. I now watch as everyone approaches the altar. And I remember that God looks on each of these people—the young, the old, the wobbly, the strong, the cranky, the spirited, the one struggling with addiction, the one enduring a divorce, the one celebrating a new job, the one mourning a friend who died—and loves every one of them. When I witness the multiplicity of people whom God loves with self-giving love, I better understand God's love for me, and I am better equipped to love that wonderful multiplicity of people in return.

I also look for love amid my everyday life. I return to 1 Corinthians 13: *Love is patient, love is kind. It does not envy, it does not boast, it is not proud . . .* Remembering this description of love helps me see God's love at work in unexpected places. When I hear that my friend's father gently dressed his mother, who was diagnosed with Alzheimer's, every morning, I receive a picture of God's love. When Penny reaches her hand out to me after I snap at her, I am humbled again in the face of love. When I read about a young Orthodox Jewish man who invited a renowned white supremacist for Shabbat dinner and the transformational friendship they share, I remember the power of love.[4] When I read the story of a Black man who has been wrongfully imprisoned and sentenced to death for a murder he did not commit leading a book club with a white man who is a former KKK member and how they came to care for one another, I believe that love is real and can be found among us all.[5] When I bear witness to any act of love in the world, regardless of whether it has any religious or Christian nature, I see God's love in action, and it expands my understanding of the breadth of that love.

Finally, we receive the love of God when we practice loving other people. Certainly there are times when caring for others simply depletes us. But there are also times when, as we give love, we also begin to understand love better. When Grand Penny was diagnosed with liver cancer, I found myself, a twenty-five-year-old newlywed, taking care of this other person in a very physical way. Grand Penny had a wound from an incision that ran from her breastbone to her bellybutton. She had tubes protruding from her side, draining pus and bile and blood. The wound needed cleaning and the tubes needed to be emptied a few times a day. Her hair and body needed washing. I found I was going to be either repulsed by it all or I would draw closer in love for her. I was going to either judge her body in its vulnerability and pain or care for it with tenderness and awe at the privilege entrusted to me. As I heard her stories and tended those wounds, I grew in my compassion toward her and all the choices she had made along the way. I grew in hope for her. And I grew in my understanding of God's expansive love and how that love could include all our mistakes and all our fears and all our selfishness and all our dreams.

God loves us like a mother holding the hand of a feverish child in the middle of the night. Like a dad lying in bed with a son writhing in pain from an earache. Like a daughter-in-law wiping the sweat from her mother-in-law's brow. When we offer that type of love to others, when we receive that love from others, we enter into the love of God for all God's children.

The foundation of reality is an unending dance of love between Father, Son, and Spirit. We have been invited into that reality, both through direct experiences of prayer and through indirect experiences of loving and being loved by one another. Like the bleeding woman and Jairus, once we are able to see our need, and once we are able to ask for help, we can receive the love of Jesus.

We are constantly invited into the healing love of God.

CHAPTER 12

Communal Healing

Go in peace and be freed from your suffering.
—MARK 5:34

When the anthropologist Margaret Mead talked about what signaled the advent of human civilization, she didn't cite the creation of tools or the use of fire. She didn't point to evidence of artistic expression. She said researchers can mark civilization's beginning through femurs that had broken and healed.[1] In those prehistoric days, to break a femur meant death, unless the rest of the nomadic group was willing to stop and care for the one with the broken bone. The only way for a femur to heal was through the generosity, compassion, and sacrifice of the other humans. For Mead, the sign of humanity was not invincibility or independence or intelligence. The sign of humanity was a collective decision to care for the broken. The sign of humanity was communal participation in healing.

Healing is not a solitary endeavor. The healing stories throughout the Gospels point to the collective nature of being made well. When the bleeding woman comes to Jesus, he restores her to her community by publicly calling her *Daughter*, and then he sends her forth: "Go in peace and be freed from your suffering." At the same time, her community experiences its own healing if and as they receive her. Time and again, when Jesus heals people, he sends them back to their family, their town, and their religious group. Healing is not complete without community.

The gospel stories offer details of individual experiences of healing and particular encounters with Jesus that occupy short moments in time, but they point us beyond the individual and toward the wider work of healing that Jesus came to offer. After Jesus heals the bleeding woman, after he restores her to herself, to God, and to her community, he sends her out with the words "Go in peace." This phrase sounds simple, and we can easily skip past its significance. But when Jesus sends her out in peace, he is referring to the Jewish concept of shalom, a word whose meaning extends far beyond our modern understanding of peace.

Shalom doesn't merely connote the absence of violence or anxiety. Rather, shalom is the presence of God in all God's goodness and beauty and generosity and love. Shalom is a vision of what the world should be. As Walter Brueggemann writes, "[Shalom] is well-being of a very personal kind . . . but it is also deliberately corporate. If there is to be well-being, it will not be just for isolated, insulated individuals; it is rather security and prosperity granted to a whole community."[2] Or as Lisa Sharon Harper puts it, "Shalom is what the Kingdom of God smells like. . . . It's when everyone has enough. It's when families are healed. It's when shame is renounced and inner freedom is laid hold of. It's when human dignity, bestowed by the image of God in all humanity, is cultivated, protected, and served in families, faith communities, and schools and through public policy."[3] Shalom is a vision of human flourishing that includes the individual but extends beyond any one person to the entire community and society. When Jesus tells this woman to go in peace, he offers a blessing. He offers hope for her continued healing. He also exhorts her to carry with her the healing she has experienced. This woman is invited to participate in her own healing, and then she is sent forth to bring healing into the world. She is invited to participate in God's larger vision of a world restored to beauty, goodness, and truth.

After Jairus and his wife watch Jesus raise their daughter back to life, they too are invited to participate in healing. In contrast to the broad directive to "go in peace," they are given a small, immediate task. Jesus turns to them and tells them to "give her something to eat" (Mark 5:43). That's the end of the story. We never hear about Jairus, his daughter, or the bleeding woman again. After two miracles and the high drama of both scenes, Mark ends this narrative with a mundane instruction to feed a child. And yet here, too, we see Jesus giving these parents a way to reconnect with their daughter, a way to serve her, a simple way to participate in a larger work of healing.

As with these figures in the Gospels, Jesus gives each of us ways to participate in a larger work of healing. We are invited to overcome the barriers of distraction, shame, and anxiety through a personal experience of God's healing love. We are also invited to overcome the barriers of social status and injustice by living out that love within our own social contexts. We are invited to go in peace, to offer food and shelter and care, to bring shalom into our own communities. For Jesus, and for us today, shalom begins with justice.

When I think of justice, I typically think of punishing wrongdoing. But in the Bible, the word *justice* refers to much more than punishment. Preacher and author Timothy Keller explains that there are two types of justice: retributive and remunerative. Retributive justice is the kind that punishes people for bad behavior and evil deeds. Remunerative justice is the kind that gives people what they need. This type of justice can take the form of providing direct assistance to people through efforts like food banks, and it can look like indirect systemic change through public policy and social programs. One example of remunerative justice comes through a nonprofit called Love Heals. This ministry, founded by Rev. Becca Stevens, exists for women who were victims of sexual abuse and trafficking. Love Heals gives—free of charge—employment and housing and healthcare and therapy and pretty much whatever support a woman needs for two years. During those years, the women work together to make and sell lotions and soaps and oils. Their products speak a message of beauty and hope for bodies that have been wounded by the weight of sin. This type of remunerative justice, writes Keller, is "far more prominent in Scripture than [God's] retributive justice."[4] Justice in the Bible is primarily a call to proactively care for those who are vulnerable.

Dominique Gilliard, another pastor and author, writes that "restoration, not punitive punishment, is at the heart of God's justice." As Gilliard puts it, "Biblically, justice is a divine act of reparation where breached relationships are renewed and victims, offenders, and communities are restored."[5] In the state of Vermont, the Department of Corrections funds a statewide network of community justice centers that help support people who have recently been released from prison. Journalist Gina Barton writes about the effects of the relationships that have developed between families and formerly incarcerated men when they have provided support in the wake of imprisonment: "Just one in 30 sex offenders involved in Circles [of Support and Accountability] was reconvicted of a felony, compared with roughly one in five of those not involved—a reduction of 86 percent. For violent offenders who had not committed sex crimes, the reduction was 80 percent."[6] This program in Vermont was modeled after a similar program in Canada started by a Mennonite pastor who called upon his congregation to befriend a man who had been released from prison after conviction for child sex offenses. Remunerative justice relies on relationships of mutual and ongoing care within local communities.

Pastor Rich Villodas offers another take on how people of faith should understand justice. He writes, "Justice very simply is about having right relationships, one with another. To do justice means that every person is taken seriously as a human being made in the image of God."[7] When Jesus sends this woman out in peace/shalom, he does so with a framework shaped entirely through the Jewish Scriptures with a comprehensive vision of justice as proactive, ongoing, communal care for every human being made in God's image.

Justice is about looking out for the needs of people who will otherwise (and often through no fault of their own) be oppressed and marginalized and downtrodden. Scholars refer to the "quartet of the vulnerable" who are lifted up on page after page in the Bible: widows, orphans, immigrants, and "the poor," which is a term that referred both to those in economic distress and to social outcasts. To do the work of justice is to look out for the needs of people who are particularly vulnerable, to advocate and act alongside them, and when they are denied a voice, to advocate and act on their behalf.

This work of justice, this work of bringing peace into the world, this work of participating in a wider social healing, parallels the work of healing within our individual lives. It emerges out of who God is as a God of love. At the heart of the universe is a relational God whose essence is love. When we are invited into that love, we receive a gift intended not only for our own benefit. We receive an invitation to an ongoing work of loving participation as we bring love into the world.

Jesus underscores the importance of love during his final teaching to his closest followers in John 15. First, Jesus instructs his disciples to "remain" in his love. This idea of remaining in love runs parallel to Paul's encouragement to be rooted in love. Trees remain in one place, even as they grow and change. Jesus exhorts us all to stay in God's presence, to receive that personal nourishment and connection and stability, to live every day in love.

Jesus follows this exhortation with what sounds like a bit of a caveat: "If you keep my commands, you will remain in my love" (John 15:10). It sounds as if he's saying, *If* you behave yourself, then I'm going to love you. *If* you get everything right, then you will also get my love. But we know from other parts of the Gospels that Jesus has pretty harsh words for people who follow religious rules, including moral rules, without grace for one another. And we know from Jesus' interactions with tax collectors, prostitutes, and other people labeled "sinners" that he does not base his own acceptance and love of people on their moral or religious behavior. Jesus goes on to say, "My command is this: Love each other" (v. 12).

It took me a while to understand the progression of Jesus' thoughts in this passage. I'm schooled in trying to earn love and approval, so I interpreted his words in a conditional way. But then I slowed down to think about what Jesus is actually saying here. The way to remain in Jesus' love is to obey his commands. His one command is to love each other. In other words, the way to remain in love is to practice love. The way to remain in love is to live lives of love.

It's a consistent message throughout the Bible. Early on in the Jewish Scriptures, followers of Yahweh are given a command that came to be called the Shema: they must love the Lord their God with all their heart, and with all their mind, and with all their soul, and with all their strength (see Deuteronomy 6:5). The unifying purpose and sign of obedience for the Jewish people was loving God with their whole selves. Centuries later, when a Jewish lawyer asks what Jesus considers to be the greatest commandment, Jesus replies with the Shema, this integrated expression of human love for God. Jesus follows up by adding, "And the second [greatest commandment] is like it: 'Love your neighbor as yourself'" (Matthew 22:39).

Jesus' healing is an invitation for people to come into the presence of God with their whole selves—heart, mind, soul, and strength. It is an invitation to receive and reflect the love of God with their whole selves. And, Jesus insists, this love for God is "like" the love we must have for our neighbor.

Perhaps when Jesus says that this second commandment is "like" the first, he simply means they are alike in their significance. What matters most to God is that we love God and love our neighbors. But it is also possible that Jesus wants us to make a connection between the character and being of God and the character and being of the person who lives next door. He might be saying, as one Jesuit scholar did, "God is the person you're talking to, the one right in front of you."[8] By this interpretation, the messy, inconvenient, often unreciprocated, little-acknowledged act of loving your neighbor is just like offering your whole self in devotion to the Creator of heaven and earth. It is a radical thought, but it is also a thought in keeping with Jesus' other statements about what it looks like to love God. In Matthew 25, Jesus says that if we feed the hungry, clothe the naked, and welcome the stranger, we offer our love to Jesus, who is one with God. When the apostle Paul sums up what matters to God, he doesn't even mention loving God directly. He simply writes, "For the entire law is fulfilled in keeping this one command: 'Love your neighbor as yourself'" (Galatians 5:14). To love God is to love our neighbor. To love our neighbor is to love God. We remain in love, we stay connected to Jesus, we continue to heal, through love.

Still, for those of us who want to participate in this healing love of Jesus two thousand years later, vague instructions to love don't carry us very far. But homing in on the very specific instructions that Jesus offers in Matthew 25, alongside the countless times God exhorts the Israelites to care for the most vulnerable people in their midst, helps us see what love looks like to God. We can argue forever about how to live out these ideals in politics or education or even churches. But bringing the shalom of God into our social realities will mean addressing injustice by proactively caring for people in need.

I don't pretend to have cracked the code on overcoming systemic injustice or creating equity in schools or the legal system or hiring practices. I do know that God invites me to bumble my way into participation in social healing in the same way that God invites me to bumble my way into practices of personal healing. Jesus sends both the healed woman and Jairus into their respective communities with instructions for participation in a wider work of healing. He invites us to do the same.

These two interrelated aspects of Jesus' healing mission have not always been wed within the church. In many historically white Protestant churches, a "personal relationship with Christ" has been pitted against the call of the "social gospel." I lived on the "personal relationship" side of this history for many years. When I worked for a Christian ministry introducing high school kids to matters of faith, it didn't cross my mind to connect the invitation to follow Jesus with confronting injustice. But for Jesus, the personal and the social are mutually reinforcing aspects of the loving character of God.

In recent years, I have begun to recognize the integral relationship between personal and social healing. At first, I saw them as a progression. I thought that personal healing came first, and then and only then would I be equipped to offer that same healing to the world. In my mind, participating in social healing came in response only to what I had already experienced. There's some truth here. As the old saying goes, "Hurt people hurt people." If I don't admit the ways in which I have sustained hurt, and if I refuse to bring that hurt to Jesus, if I instead skip ahead and try to bring love and peace and justice into the world around me, I can easily harm others. Yet I've also learned that our participation in social healing is a part of our personal healing.

As an able-bodied, educated, affluent white woman, I grew up functionally estranged from all sorts of people whose bodies and backgrounds were different from mine. I went to school with other people like me. I scampered around the church graveyard after the service with other kids like me. I was surrounded by kids like me at camp, ballet class, piano recitals. And once I was an adult, everyone around me looked more or less the same at restaurants, on vacation, in neighborhoods. I lived within a homogenous world that didn't even hint at the beautiful diversity of God's creation. Part of my own personal healing was to look for bridges that spanned the social divides, that enabled me to bring my gifts and resources to people who had been cut off from the opportunities I had been given while simultaneously receiving the gifts they had to offer me. In making connections with people of different racial and ethnic backgrounds, in serving people with disabilities and receiving the gifts of their ministry, in learning about different social perspectives—in all these ways and more, I have seen the impoverishment of my own soul, and I have begun to both receive and participate in healing.

In his sermon about Jesus' parable of the good Samaritan, Dr. Martin Luther King Jr. reflects on the significance of a Samaritan going out of his way, at the risk of his own life, to help a badly wounded Jewish man. King argues that this kindness on the Samaritan's part is not merely an act of altruism. Rather, by acting across the boundary lines of ethnic and religious categories, the Samaritan is also participating in his own healing, and the mutual healing of their respective communities. As King writes, "In the final analysis, I must not ignore the wounded man on life's Jericho Road, because he is a part of me and I am a part of him. His agony diminishes me, and his salvation enlarges me."[9]

Multiple healing stories in the Gospels hint at the reciprocal nature of healing, at how it blesses both the individual and the society. Individuals can bring healing to others and receive it at the same time. There's the story of the ten lepers who come to Jesus crying out for help. Jesus indeed "cleanses" them, and he sends them on their way to the priests. Later, one of them returns to give thanks to Jesus. Luke makes two points here. One, that the one who gave thanks was "saved/healed," whereas the nine men who did not give thanks were simply cleansed. Two, Luke highlights this man's ethnicity: "and he was a Samaritan" (Luke 17:16). Jesus' work of healing is not simply for Jewish people, but rather for the healing of a nation that splintered long ago into factions, including the division of Jew and Samaritan.

Bryan Stevenson, author of *Just Mercy* and director of the Equal Justice Initiative, tells a modern version of how social and personal healing intertwine. Part of Stevenson's work has been to create the Legacy Museum in Montgomery, Alabama. This narrative museum bears witness to the United States' long history of racism and dehumanization of Black people from the days of slavery through the era of Jim Crow through the modern injustices of mass incarceration. In one section of the Legacy Museum stands a wall of glass jars filled with dirt from locations around the country where individuals were murdered through lynching. The names of the victims and the locations of the murders are printed on the individual jars.

Stevenson tells the story of a Black woman who volunteered to collect dirt. She was kneeling at the side of the road, ready to put soil in her jar, when a white man in a pickup truck pulled over and asked what she was doing. Though she felt afraid, she explained. He asked if he could join in her work. Stevenson recounted the story to journalist Terry Gross:

> And then she told me that this white man got on his knees. And she offered him the little plow to dig the soil. And he said, no, no, no. You use that.
>
> And he started throwing his hands into the soil with such force. And his hands were getting coated with this black soil. . . . She said the next thing she knew, she had tears running down her face. And he stopped and he said, oh, I'm so sorry I'm upsetting you. And she said, no, no, no, no. You're blessing me. . . . And she noticed toward the end that the man was slowing down and that his shoulders were shaking. . . . And she saw the man had tears running down his face, and she stopped. And she put her hand on

this man's shoulder. She said, are you all right? And that's when the man said to her, he said, no. I'm just so worried that it might have been my grandparents that were involved in lynching this man. And she said, they both sat there with tears running down their face.

And at the end of it, he stood up and said, I want to take a picture of you holding the jar. And she said, I want to take a picture of you holding the jar. And they both took pictures holding the jar. And she brought this man back, and they put that jar on our exhibit together. Now, beautiful things like that don't always happen when you tell the truth about history, when you try to actually look for redemption and restoration, when you have every reason to be afraid and angry. But until we commit to some acts like that, until we tell the truth, we deny ourselves the beauty of redemption, the beauty of restoration.[10]

Both that man and that woman, as well as their families, their communities, and everyone who heard about that moment, experienced some measure of healing through their shared experience.

When Jesus sends out this woman he calls *Daughter*, it is not because her healing is complete and she is now ready to offer a helping hand to others. It is because there is healing yet ahead for her in reconnecting to her people. And it is because there is healing yet ahead for the community in receiving her and, perhaps, in recognizing the possibility of receiving others like her who have been shunned or shamed or outcast.

When God's healing begins in our lives, we too are sent forth in peace, to bring justice, to bring proactive care to hurting people and communities. We too are sent forth to live in love.

CHAPTER 13

Social Healing

After [Jesus] put them all out, he took the child's father and mother and the disciples who were with him, and went in where the child was. He took her by the hand and said to her, *"Talitha koum!"* (which means, "Little girl, I say to you, get up!").

Immediately the girl stood up and began to walk around (she was twelve years old). At this they were completely astonished. He gave strict orders not to let anyone know about this, and told them to give her something to eat.

—MARK 5:40–43

The sound of plates and bowls and glasses shattering probably lasted for less than a minute, but it seemed to go on forever. Peter and I were in our second year of marriage. We had just moved into our first house, a one-bedroom bungalow on the north side of Richmond, Virginia. In preparing to welcome a guest for dinner, I had removed a large serving bowl from our new china cabinet. Moving the bowl created an empty space on the middle shelf, so I repositioned a stack of china plates to fill in the gap. I closed the glass doors to the cabinet and returned to the kitchen, satisfied with the way it all looked. And then we heard a thump. And then the shattering.

The plates on that middle shelf had been too heavy. They not only caused the shelf to collapse, but made it tilt forward. The contents of the middle shelf pushed the doors open, and all the china fell and became a mound of green and white shards. The glasses and bowls on the bottom shelf lay in pieces on the floor.

I worked in youth ministry at the time, so after the shock and loss wore off, I saw the whole experience as a fitting analogy for the human condition. A modern-day Humpty Dumpty. As humans, we've fallen apart. And we can't put ourselves back together again. I still have a small box of that china, with its jagged edges reminding me how quickly something precious and beautiful can break into pieces.

But I no longer think of that china as a great analogy for the human condition. Yes, each and every one of us carries wounded and broken places within our souls, and we cannot put ourselves back together on our own. And yes, on a communal level, our society has splintered into warring factions, and those cannot be repaired solely through human effort either. Still, Jesus' healing work shows me that brokenness is not the beginning or the end of the story of our individual lives or our communities. There is more to the plot than shattered glass.

For Christians, the most glorious image of humanity and the most beautiful portrait of love comes in the resurrected body of Jesus. His broken, and healed, body is the place of hope and power and life and promise. The gospel writers tell us that Jesus offers his body as the way of salvation, the way of healing.

Jesus does not heal or save himself as he hangs upon the cross. He receives the wounds of beating and crucifixion. He allows his body to shatter with the brokenness of the world. A few days later, after he has been raised from the dead, Jesus appears to his disciples. At first, they think he is a ghost. But he wants them to understand that he has returned in a real body. To make it clear, he says: "Look at my hands and my feet" (Luke 24:39). He doesn't say, "Look at my nose," or "Come touch my kneecap." In order for the disciples to know who he is, Jesus draws their attention not to his physical body in a general way, but to the particular places where he has been wounded and healed.

In this moment, Jesus demonstrates that he is not a ghost. But he does much more than that. It is through awareness of his scars that his disciples know the nature of his resurrected humanity. He turns their attention to the places where his body had been broken and now has been restored and even transformed. He turns their attention to the abuse that has been forgiven but not forgotten. He turns their attention to the place of harm, which is also the place of healing. They are not supposed to ignore or forget the horror of what happened. Rather, they are supposed to see the way God can redeem and restore wholeness even to a broken body, the way God can piece together a shattered self, the way God brings healing through the power of love.

Many years after all those plates fell out of our china cabinet, I learned about the Japanese tradition of *kintsugi*. As Makoto Fujimura, a Japanese American Christian and visual artist, has explained, kintsugi emerged from Japanese tea ceremonies. On the occasion when a piece of exquisite pottery shattered, the people did not leave the pottery in pieces. Rather, artisans took the shards and glued them back together with lacquer mixed with gold. Their art drew attention to the broken places as they pieced together the cups and bowls and pots with precious materials. In mending the broken places with gold, they made something even more beautiful.

Fujimura sees kintsugi as a cultural parable that offers us a way to understand how God heals. In his book *Art + Faith*, Fujimura writes, "By honoring the brokenness, the broken shapes can somehow be a necessary component of the New World to come."[1] The beauty comes not by trying to cover over or ignore the brokenness, but by transforming the brokenness. Like Jesus' resurrection scars, this practice of kintsugi does not erase brokenness, nor does it separate brokenness and beauty. It offers us an image of what the work of repair might look like within our own bodies and within our own culture.

Like the artisans who were able to see the inherent beauty even within a broken vessel, we need to be able to see the truth and goodness and beauty inherent within our individual lives and inherent within our life together. Instead of seeing shards and fragments and divided factions, God invites us to see our own belovedness and the belovedness of all God's good creation. We are invited to acknowledge the brokenness so that we can participate in transforming that brokenness, participate in bringing forth that beauty and blessing. God invites us to join in the Spirit's healing work.

In *The Life of the Beloved*, Henri Nouwen describes the process we all go through to understand our belovedness. He explains that we are all broken people who are also chosen and blessed by God. He goes on to write, "The great spiritual call of the Beloved Children of God is to pull their brokenness away from the shadow of the curse and put it under the light of the blessing."[2] The resurrected body of Jesus—still bearing the scars of crucifixion—offers an image of bringing brokenness under blessing. These are the scars that bear witness to God's love for the entire world. These are the scars that invite us to acknowledge our own personal and collective brokenness and bring that brokenness under the blessing of God.

Throughout the Gospels, Jesus gives us picture after picture of what it looks like to bring our brokenness under the blessing of God. Sometimes this takes the form of miraculous healing, where a dead child is restored to life or a woman immediately stops bleeding. But those were the unusual stories then, and they are the unusual stories now.

We see Jesus healing people in the Gospels, but we also see Jesus loving people exactly as they are and bringing blessing into their brokenness. We encounter a woman who weeps at Jesus' feet. Without any demonstrable change in her life circumstances, Jesus tells her that her faith has made her well, and he sends her out with his blessing. In Luke 14, when Jesus describes who will sit together with God at the heavenly banquet, he lists the lame and the poor and the blind as the ones who will come to the table first. He doesn't list all the people who have experienced bodily healing. He doesn't list the rich and powerful. He lists the ones who are in pain and bewildered and bedraggled. He asks us to imagine them feasting with God. And Jesus' list of people who can know God's blessing here and now is a list that includes the poor, the ones in mourning, the meek, and the ones who are hated (Matthew 5:1–11).

Each of us comes to Jesus from our own particular places of brokenness and wounding. Each of us will receive some measure of healing that we can carry out into the world even as the scars from those wounded places remain. We can bring our sin and our shame, our perfectionism, addictions, distractions, and heartaches to God. We can bring our history of racism and injustice and dehumanization and disregard for God's good creation. And as we do, we will receive healing, and we will be sent forth to be agents of God's ongoing healing work, God's faithful work of repair in all the broken places of our hearts and our communities. On a personal level, we are welcomed into God's family and restored to our own belovedness. We are also sent forth to create and inhabit spaces of belonging, spaces of shalom.

Before Penny was born, I hadn't thought much about belonging. But in the first few years of her life, there were obvious times when she did not belong. There was the preschool director who rejected her without meeting her, the playdates where other kids could run around and she didn't have the physical ability to participate, the dance class where she was encouraged to eat snacks in the lobby because she couldn't "keep up" with the rest of the students. And there were more subtle cues that people saw Penny as out of place in our society—the comments I received about my courage when I became pregnant again, the times people looked past Penny and asked me questions about her as if she weren't there, the derogatory remarks made in Hollywood and by politicians about people with intellectual disabilities.

But my years as Penny's mom have also given me eyes to see what belonging looks like. We are part of a church that is just as likely to invite Penny to read scripture as any other member of the congregation. Once, it was Penny's turn to read when a guest preacher came to town. He sent the week's passages ahead of time, without knowing that a child with Down syndrome would be reading Psalm 139 from the pulpit. For all of us, to hear Penny proclaim "I am fearfully and wonderfully made" only underlined the point that we are all welcomed and valued by God. Because Penny belonged to our community, we all received a message from her about our place of belonging within God's family.

There was also the time Penny received a diagnosis of scoliosis and the sobering news that she would need to wear a restrictive plastic brace that surrounded her torso and squeezed her back into alignment for twenty hours a day. I cried the first time I strapped her into it. On a very practical level, because of the brace, none of her old clothes would fit anymore. When I told my family the news, one of my sisters said with confidence, "I guess we need to have a party!" They all arrived with new clothes for Penny. They turned a hardship into a fashion show. They turned what could have felt shameful into a mark of distinction. They made sure Penny knew how much she belonged.

Belonging happens when each member of a community is so crucial to the health and wholeness of the community that the community aches from any member's absence. Belonging happens when each individual is one critical component of an interdependent whole. Belonging happens when "we aren't us without you," when your presence is integral to our identity.[3]

Belonging matters for all of us, and especially for those who historically have been excluded and marginalized from institutional spaces—people with disabilities, mental health concerns, addictions; people who live in poverty; people from racial and ethnic backgrounds that do not conform to the ideals of "whiteness." Skylar Mitchell wrote an essay for the *New York Times* about her decision as a Black woman to attend a historically Black college, Spelman, instead of Swarthmore, a historically white institution. Both colleges are prestigious, but Swarthmore ranks higher according to official national metrics. Mitchell described walking around Spelman, where she would be required to learn about the contributions of Black men and women to our nation. She would sit in lecture halls and classrooms where she felt confident her perspective would be received rather than minimized. She writes, "There is something powerful about attending an institution that was built for you."[4]

What would it look like to build and reform our institutional spaces to communicate a message of belonging that extends beyond one homogenous group that has always gathered there? If a church places a wheelchair-accessible ramp at the back entrance of the building with a dumpster nearby, the architecture itself might comply with regulations for accessibility, but it communicates exclusion. If a school has an open admission policy for all applicants but lines the hallways with photographs of only white men, the space communicates exclusion. Before cities had "curb cuts," small inclines to allow wheels to move from street to sidewalk and back again, the cityscape communicated who belonged.

Belonging is more than a matter of architecture and photographs, of course, and belonging can happen without fancy or expensive remodeling of buildings—although a willingness to transform physical spaces, sacrifice time and money, and change the status quo in order to welcome new people is often necessary too. Belonging ultimately rests on a posture of the heart. It depends on whether a community is prepared not only to welcome a diverse array of individuals but also to be transformed through relationships of mutual giving and receiving.

What healing could happen if churches became communities that do not reflect typical social stratification? What political actions might we take to reform our schools, our justice system, our social services? What might we be willing to risk, to lose, for the sake of our communal healing?

Most of our communal life—both within the church and within our society—shows signs of brokenness more than belonging. We carry with us a history of exclusion and discrimination, from social clubs and private schools and denominational policies to legal systems and medical practices that divided us into separate racial and economic communities. Like plates shattered on the floor, we need to be pieced back together again to experience collective healing and to serve a common purpose. We also need a vision of the newness, the beauty, the exquisite creative expression that such healing could engender.

My friend David Bailey has pointed out that we can't move quickly or easily from spaces of exclusion to spaces of belonging. David is a Black man who grew up in Richmond, Virginia, where the shadows of Confederate monuments literally hovered over the main streets of the city alongside hundreds of racially segregated churches proclaiming Jesus as Lord. David now leads a nonprofit organization called Arrabon that helps institutions become reconciling communities.

David gave me a vision of an in-between space—a space of healing, a space for the creative work of piecing back together broken places with beauty—when he invited me to join him at a songwriting workshop for the Porter's Gate Project. For this workshop, about forty Christian songwriters came together to write songs based on scripture about justice.

Participants were white, Black, Asian, Latinx. They flew in from around the country. Male and female. Catholic and Protestant. Elderly and young. But they shared a common faith and a common purpose. And they gathered in a space that didn't belong to any of them. No one had power or familiarity. They simply had the common cause of creating something out of their own giftedness for the sake of the church.

At the end of our time together, David talked with the whole group about three "tables" within American Christianity. The first table was a white one. As a Black man, he has been invited to the white table on many occasions. He's even felt appreciated and listened to there. But he is always a guest, invited to assimilate to the norms of that group in order to stay at the table. The second table was for people of color. In his experience, that meant connecting with people within the historic Black church, home to millions of faithful witnesses to the power of Jesus to liberate our bodies and souls from the bondage of slavery and sin and death—that table provides a safe and necessary space for Black Christians. The third table, David said, was a collaborative one, a table where no group of people has overt dominance. Where ideas are freely exchanged with mutual submission and respect. And where Christians truly can overcome theological and social differences in order to serve a common cause. In Nashville that weekend, a table of true collaboration was created. And that space provided a beautiful, nourishing feast.[5]

It's a stretch to claim that the bleeding woman or Jairus left that encounter with Jesus and began to think about how they could create communities of belonging. And yet bringing Jesus' words of shalom into our contemporary context requires that we harness our spiritual imaginations and consider what it would look like to take God's commands seriously to do justice, to love our neighbors, and to live in unity together. Creating collaborative spaces that allow diverse groups of people to come together with a common cause is one step toward communal healing. One step toward bringing our historic brokenness under the beautiful and generative blessing of God, that we might be given—together—to the world, in love. Perhaps one day we will be able to look back and see that what once was broken has been brought together with gold and made more beautiful in the process.

We need to pursue the work of piecing together communities through collaborative experiences and opportunities. We need to acknowledge the ongoing harm of injustice and participate in undoing it. But Jesus' call does not stop with collaboration or even with undoing injustice. Jesus insists on full belonging for all people at the table of God. Jesus insists on claiming the ones most likely to be marginalized as those who belong at the celebratory feast in God's eternal presence.

Throughout his ministry, Jesus teaches belonging: The parable of the good Samaritan claims that the religious heretic belongs. The parable of the sheep and the goats teaches that the prisoner and the homeless wanderer belong. The parable of the wedding banquet insists that the physically disabled belong, as they are. The Beatitudes proclaim that the poor, those in positions of both economic and social disadvantage, belong. The widow. The foreigner. The racial and ethnic other. They belong in the family of God (see Luke 10:25–37; Matthew 25:31–46; Luke 14:15–24; and Matthew 5:1–12, respectively). Jesus teaches this truth again and again and again.

Jesus also lives out this ethos when he welcomes little children onto his lap, when he welcomes women as his disciples, and in his many moments of offering God's healing presence to individuals on the margins. For any community to become a place of belonging that reflects the wideness of the family of God, for any community that wants to welcome, like Jesus, the ones typically scorned or ignored by society—uncomfortable change is crucial. Healing work includes undoing systems of oppression, divesting power, sharing resources, confessing sin, and lamenting injustice.

In the story of the bleeding woman, at first, her transformation depends on Jesus. She seeks him out in faith. He bestows power. He names her *Daughter*. But social healing depends on everyone else. When Jesus publicly announces that the bleeding woman has been healed, he is calling on the community to do its part to welcome her, to participate in her healing, to participate in their own healing. We need the power of God, and we need the connection and commitment to one another, to be made well.

We are all invited to understand that we have been made well by God. We have been broken by sin, the sin inherent within our own choices but also the sin that exists in the world around us. Jesus comes to piece us back together and make us into people who are even more beautiful as a result of that very brokenness. The promise of Jesus' resurrected body is that brokenness doesn't last forever. That brokenness can be made beautiful. That brokenness is not the beginning, the center, or the end of our story.

Jesus invites all of us to go to the place of the brokenness, to ask for help in that place, and to experience the beauty and blessing of being made well. Then we are free to bring that blessing, that healing, that love, into the world.

Epilogue

It's easy to read stories of miraculous physical healing and wonder why our bodies are still in pain. It's easy to hear stories of inspirational social change and feel paralyzed by inadequacy. It's easy to think that our own participation in healing will never be enough.

In their book *Reconciling All Things*, Emmanuel Katongole and Chris Rice write about how we want the work of shalom, the work of reconciliation, to be fast, innocent, and global.[1] We want healing everywhere, with ease, right now. We want the Hollywood version of justice. We want the Hallmark version of healing. I take great comfort in Katongole and Rice's reminder that in real life, reconciliation is slow, and messy, and local.

I would add *small* to their list. The work of participation in healing often begins with small, almost imperceptible or unnoticeable, certainly unremarkable steps. As Jesus says to Jairus and his wife, *Give her something to eat.* Or as he says to us:

Pray with a friend. Volunteer at a local nonprofit. Read a news story about injustice. Just as Jesus teaches that the kingdom of God is like a mustard seed or a grain of yeast, so all we need is to take small, local, messy, slow steps toward healing.

Some of the small steps we have taken as a family include diversifying the books on our children's bookshelves and extending hospitality to people from different social backgrounds from our own. We've changed the way we give money as well as the way we invest money so that we can recognize the historic injustice of the racial wealth gap and support communities of color. As a family, we've traveled to museums and memorials throughout the Southeast to understand more about the history of oppression and the fight for equal rights in our nation. We've also worked to uphold the inherent value of people with disabilities.

I spent years reading and watching and listening to information and stories about injustice and social divisions, but it was admitting my own helplessness and asking for God's help that made the biggest difference. I began to take small steps toward healing once I acknowledged not only the harm I participate in, but also the impossibility of fixing all the problems.

We have begun a lifelong journey of trusting in God's healing love for ourselves and for our communities. It is slow, small, and messy. It will most likely go unnoticed. But it is also our way of participating in God's ongoing work of love.

I sat on a yoga mat and received physical healing seven years ago. That moment opened up a pathway toward a deeper healing that led first to a new awareness of my own woundedness, my own shame and hurt and anger and grief. And then that moment opened up a pathway to my own belovedness. And then to the healing love available to each of us and to all of us and the invitation for me to participate in it.

In Romans 5:5, Paul writes that "hope does not put us to shame, because God's love has been poured out into our hearts through the Holy Spirit." It's as if this vast waterfall of love cascades into the wounded places within our own souls, and over time, we find that there is more than enough love and that God will keep pouring it into us, and around us, forever. Love that fills us to overflowing. Love that moves like water, seeping into every broken place, every crack and crevice, love that works its way into our personal places of shame and pain and heartache. Love that flows from us into our community's areas of shame and pain without leaving us parched and thirsty for more. Abundant, transformative, healing love, flowing down and through us, washing us and restoring us and strengthening us and blessing us.

When I look back on this story of Jesus with the bleeding woman, with Jairus and his daughter, and with so many other people who experienced pain and disability and mental illness and grief and fear and shame and loss—I am reminded again of the intimacy of every one of these encounters. Jesus receives each of them as they are. He listens. He touches them with gentle reassurance. He restores them with the tenderness of a word like *daughter*. Jesus also sends each of them back out into the world to bring that healing love wherever they go.

Healing is not a performance. Healing is not an achievement. Healing is not a reward. Healing is not a requirement. Healing is a gift of grace. A gift of love for each of us and for all of us. And there is so much love.

Acknowledgments

Once a week, I sit down with other women and talk about a passage from the Bible. Over the years, we've read passages from the Gospels. We've read portions of Genesis and Psalms. We've considered Ephesians and Philippians and Colossians. Sometimes these groups have consisted of three other people, other times a dozen. Sometimes we've met in person. and other times on Zoom. But in every case, I have been challenged and comforted and blessed to wrestle through questions and doubts and fears, to learn new truths about who God is, and to walk together through the hardships and joys of this life. I wrote this book for the women and girls who have gathered with me to ask honest questions and offer vulnerable concerns and learn and grow together. I wrote this book for you, with tremendous thanks for the ways you have nourished and anchored and connected me to the love of God throughout these many years.

I am also thankful to the Coasters (Patricia, Doli, Heidi, Elizabeth, and Sarah), and to Katherine and Kiersten for reading portions of this manuscript, and for listening (so much listening!) as I wrestled through the writing process. Niro, Tracey, and Melanie—thank you for reading multiple drafts and offering insightful comments and prayers and words of encouragement. Matt, thank you for confirming that the best thing for someone without a PhD in New Testament studies is a friend with a PhD in New Testament studies! I so appreciate your help in staying true to the biblical text. Anne, thank you for helping me learn what it means to be made well.

Amber, your willingness to find data and suggest resources and provide support and encouragement at every step of the way is invaluable. I am so grateful we get to work together. Chris, you have championed this book with tireless enthusiasm for years. It truly would not exist without your encouragement and vision and support. Thank you!

Laura and the team at Herald Press, thank you for your enthusiasm and insight in shaping each chapter. You took a risk in believing we could pull together themes of personal and social healing in the midst of a global pandemic and racial reckoning, and I am grateful!

And finally, Peter, Penny, William, and Marilee. You've seen this book in action whenever I've asked you about physical symptoms that might signal spiritual distress. You've seen evidence of this healing work in my own life, in our family, and as we seek to participate in God's healing love in the world. And you've encouraged me to keep going even when it meant a disorganized household and a distracted mom. I love you. And I am forever thankful for who you are in my life.

Notes

CHAPTER 1

1. Brad S. Gregory, *The Unintended Reformation: How a Religious Revolution Secularized Society* (Cambridge, MA: The Belknap Press, 2012), 26.
2. Although English translations tell us she touched the hem of his garments, most commentators think she reached out for the tassels on Jesus' robe. Rabbis customarily wore robes with tassels, and those tassels served as reminders of God's commandments. See Numbers 15:37–42.
3. Commentators point out that Jesus asks this question using the masculine form of the Greek words. In other words, he expects it to be a man who has touched him, which makes his care for this woman all the more remarkable.
4. Barclay M. Newman, *A Concise Greek-English Dictionary of the New Testament* (Deutsche Bibelgesellschaft, 1993), 177.
5. Newman, 85, 83.

CHAPTER 2

1. James Nestor, *Breath: The New Science of a Lost Art* (New York: Riverhead Books, 2020), 205.
2. Erik Vance, *Suggestible You: The Curious Science of Your Brain's Ability to Deceive, Transform, and Heal* (Washington, DC: National Geographic, 2016), 61.
3. Melanie Warner, *The Magic Feather Effect: The Science of Alternative Medicine and the Surprising Power of Belief* (New York: Scribner, 2019), 70.
4. Vance, *Suggestible You*, 19.
5. Gabor Maté, *When the Body Says No: The Cost of Hidden Stress*, rev. ed. (Nashville: Turner Publishing, 2011), 32.

6. Sebastian White, Romanaus Cessario, Peter John Cameron, ed., *The Magnificat Advent Companion 2021* (Yonkers, NY: Magnificat, 2021), 24.

7. Bethany McKinney Fox, *Disability and the Way of Jesus: Holistic Healing in the Gospels and the Church* (Downers Grove, IL: IVP Academic, 2019), 28.

8. James R. Edwards, *The Gospel According to Luke*, Pillar New Testament Commentary (Grand Rapids: Eerdmans, 2015), 256.

9. Richard Bauckham notes that Yeshua seems to have been the sixth most common boys' name in Jesus' time.

10. My friend Matt also tells me that the best translation for *sozo* would be "deliverer," which holds a broader meaning than the physical transformation that English assumes with the word *healer* and the spiritual transformation of the English word *savior*. Others prefer the translation "rescuer." I like the clunky combination of words—healer/savior—as a way to remind myself of the breadth of the idea that Jesus is inviting our whole selves to experience and participate in his work of redemption.

11. Brian Brock, *Wondrously Wounded: Theology, Disability, and the Body of Christ* (Waco, TX: Baylor University Press, 2019), 29.

12. Jay Wolf and Katherine Wolf, *Suffer Strong: How to Survive Anything by Redefining Everything* (Grand Rapids: Zondervan Books, 2020), 172.

13. Kyle Stevenson, "Finding Healing in My Disability," *Reflections*, Fall 2021, https://reflections.yale.edu/article/divine-access-disability-and-belonging/finding-healing-my-disability. Quotation from Kathy Black, *A Healing Homiletic: Preaching and Disability* (Nashville: Abingdon Press, 1996), 48–51.

14. Kate Bowler, *No Cure for Being Human (and Other Truths I Need to Hear)* (New York: Random House, 2021), 174–75.

CHAPTER 3

1. John Swinton, foreword to *Disability and the Way of Jesus: Holistic Healing in the Gospels and the Church*, by Bethany McKinney Fox (Downers Grove, IL: IVP Academic, 2019), x.

2. Swinton, x. Emphasis in the original.

3. This woman also would have been considered ceremonially unclean. She would not have been permitted to worship in the temple, and other people who touched her would also be ceremonially unclean. That said, modern scholars disagree about whether her status would have prevented her from interacting with others in everyday life, since they worshiped in the temple only on feast days. See Matthew Thiessen, *Jesus and the Forces of Death: The Gospels' Portrayal of Ritual Impurity within First-Century Judaism* (Grand Rapids: Baker, 2021).

4. See, for example, that Jesus looks at a rich man and loves him in Mark 10:21, looks at the crowd of hungry people and feels compassion in Mark 6:34, and grieves with Mary at Lazarus' tomb in John 11:35.

5. Modern Christians usually refer to this as "the Lord's Prayer," which we say as a slightly altered compilation of Matthew 6:9–13 and Luke 11:2–4.

6. Multiple parables place God in the role of father, including—and most famously—Luke 15:11–32. And although Jesus makes a point of welcoming literal little children, he also makes a point of calling his own disciples little children at various points throughout the Gospels.

7. Janet Martin Soskice, *The Kindness of God: Metaphor, Gender, and Religious Language* (Oxford: Oxford University Press, 2007), 75.

8. Nouwen writes about this experience in multiple books, including *Life of the Beloved, Adam,* and *Road to Daybreak.*

9. Osheta Moore, *Dear White Peacemakers: Dismantling Racism with Grit and Grace* (Harrisonburg, VA: Herald Press, 2021), 51.

10. Some of these prayers come directly from the Bible. See 1 John 4 and 1 Corinthians 13. Others are more general statements derived from biblical passages.

CHAPTER 4

1. Matthew, Mark, Luke, and John are the four "gospels" that appear in Bibles. These are the biographies of Jesus that the early church recognized as the four authoritative collections of stories and teachings that should be passed along to future generations. In recent years, many other early "gospels" have also been discovered. Scholars still debate when these gospels originated and why they were not considered Scripture by the early church. Matthew, Mark, Luke, and John have been included in the canon—the established and agreed upon books of Scripture—for centuries because of their connection to the earliest communities of Christians, their consistent witness about Jesus, and their ongoing usefulness to the church. The community of faith kept these gospels alive, even through much persecution, because they received them as God's word to the church about Jesus.

2. Bethany McKinney Fox, *Disability and the Way of Jesus: Holistic Healing in the Gospels and the Church* (Downers Grove, IL: IVP Academic, 2019), 82.

3. National Academies of Sciences, Engineering, and Medicine, *Social Isolation and Loneliness in Older Adults: Opportunities for the Health Care System* (Washington, DC: The National Academies Press, 2020), https://doi.org/10.17226/25663.

4. Bessel A. van der Kolk, *The Body Keeps the Score: Brain, Mind, and Body in the Healing of Trauma* (New York: Penguin, 2014), 212.

5. Mandy Erickson, "Alcoholics Anonymous Most Effective Path to Alcohol Abstinence," Stanford Medical School, last modified March 11, 2020, https://med.stanford.edu/news/all-news/2020/03/alcoholics-anonymous-most-effective-path-to-alcohol-abstinence.html.

6. Maria E. Pagano, Karen B. Friend, J. Scott Tonigan, and Robert L. Stout, "Helping Other Alcoholics in Alcoholics Anonymous and Drinking Outcomes: Findings from Project MATCH," *Journal of Studies on Alcohol* 65, no. 6 (2004), 766–73, https://doi.org/10.15288/jsa.2004.65.766.

7. Victoria Sweet, *God's Hotel: A Doctor, a Hospital, and a Pilgrimage to the Heart of Medicine* (New York: Riverhead Books, 2012), 39.

CHAPTER 5

1. Flannery O'Connor, "Revelation," in *Flannery O'Connor: Collected Works*, ed. Sally Fitzgerald (New York: Literary Classics of the United States, 1988), 652–54.
2. Timothy G. Gombis, *Mark: The Story of God Bible Commentary* (Grand Rapids: Zondervan Academic, 2021), 104.
3. Controversy arises once Jesus reminds people that God healed non-Israelites through the prophets Elijah and Elisha. When Jesus heals on the Sabbath, he asserts his own authority and contravenes the leaders' understanding of the laws protecting the Sabbath day.
4. I am grateful to Paul Miller's unpublished teaching on money for pointing out that God is most frequently portrayed by Jesus as a wealthy man. For more teaching from Paul Miller, see https://www.seejesus.net/.
5. Commentators often note that these words are rendered in Aramaic rather than translated into Greek. Whenever we read Aramaic in the Gospels, we retain a remnant of the earliest tradition of telling this story. Aramaic phrases show up a handful of other times, and these words take us closer than any others to the original words of Jesus.

CHAPTER 6

1. Cal Newport, *Digital Minimalism: Choosing a Focused Life in a Noisy World* (New York: Portfolio/Penguin, 2019).
2. Ruth Haley Barton, *Invitation to Silence and Solitude: Experiencing God's Transforming Presence* (Downers Grove, IL: InterVarsity Press, 2009).
3. Ruth Haley Barton, *Invitation to Retreat: The Gift and Necessity of Time Away with God* (Downers Grove, IL: InterVarsity Press, 2018), 18.
4. Anahad O'Connor, "Excessive Drinking Rose during the Pandemic. Here Are Ways to Cut Back," *New York Times*, April 12, 2021, https://www.nytimes.com/2021/04/12/well/mind/covid-pandemic-drinking.html.

CHAPTER 7

1. Research and Markets, "Anti-Aging Products Industry Projected to Be Worth $83.2 Billion by 2027—Key Trends, Opportunities and Players," GlobeNewswire News Room (Research and Markets), July 24, 2020, https://www.globenewswire.com/news-release/2020/07/24/2067180//28124/en/Anti-Aging-Products-Industry-Projected-to-be-Worth-83-2-Billion-by-2027-Key-Trends-Opportunities-and-Players.html.
2. Debra J. Brody, Jeffery P. Hughes, and Laura A. Pratt, *Prevalence of Depression among Adults Aged 20 and Over: United States, 2013–2016* (Centers for Disease Control and Prevention, February 13, 2018), https://www.cdc.gov/nchs/data/databriefs/db303.pdf.
3. Brené Brown, *Daring Greatly: How the Courage to Be Vulnerable Transforms the Way We Live, Love, Parent, and Lead* (New York: Avery/Penguin Random House, 2012), 69.
4. Curt Thompson, *The Soul of Shame: Retelling the Stories We Believe about Ourselves* (Downers Grove, IL: InterVarsity Press, 2021), 148–49.

5. Bessel A. van der Kolk, *The Body Keeps the Score: Brain, Mind, and Body in the Healing of Trauma* (New York: Penguin, 2014). Van der Kolk returns to this theme throughout the book, but chapter 2 offers his perspective on why drugs are helpful in arresting symptoms but not sufficient in healing the underlying causes of the symptoms themselves. See p. 38.
6. The text does not include the detail of Jesus placing his hands on her. I imagine it that way in light of the other times in which Jesus intentionally touches a hurting person and communicates his compassion to them.

CHAPTER 8

1. Aaron Zitner, "Working from Home Is Taking a Toll on Our Backs and Necks," *Wall Street Journal*, May 13, 2020, https://www.wsj.com/articles/working-from-home-is-taking-a-toll-on-our-backs-and-necks-11589398420.
2. Jim Wilhoit, "Quieting Your Anxious Mind," February 12, 2017, https://static1.squarespace.com/static/52be0825e4b03ae7cbd20aa2/t/587c47d3bf629abac09ad791/1484539860119/Quieting+your+anxious+Mind+%231.pdf.

CHAPTER 9

1. Wendell Berry, *The Hidden Wound* (Berkley, CA: Counterpoint, 1989), 3–4.
2. Heather McGhee, *The Sum of Us: What Racism Costs Everyone and How We Can Prosper Together* (New York: Penguin Random House, 2021), 28.
3. Tax collectors were despised by their fellow Jews because they collected money on behalf of the Roman government, akin to Nazi moles and sympathizers in occupied Europe during WWII. *Sinners* was a category of people who were unable or unwilling to follow the codes of the Torah. Later Jewish writings place both criminals and ordinary laborers like shepherds and money-lenders in that category.
4. If you are a Democrat, imagine how you would feel to see a picture of Nancy Pelosi putting her feet up and clinking glasses with a group of NRA members. If you are a Republican, imagine Mike Pence dancing and laughing with the receptionist in a Planned Parenthood waiting room.
5. Many scholars believe that Jesus wanted leaders to remember Ezekiel 34, in which the prophet excoriates the shepherds of Israel for not caring for the weak and sick and injured among them.

CHAPTER 10

1. These specific prayers come from Matthew 11:30; Philippians 4:6–7; and Ephesians 3:17b. References to the body come up throughout the Bible. The Psalms frequently refer to the sensory experience of delight and pain in the body. I offer these as examples of how the Bible can give us a way to pray through pain we experience in our bodies.
2. Mindy Roll, "How I Came to Love Embodied Prayer," *Christian Century*, June 25, 2021, https://www.christiancentury.org/article/first-person/how-i-came-love-embodied-prayer.

3. Barbara Brown Taylor, *An Altar in the World: Finding the Sacred beneath Our Feet* (New York: Harper One, 2009), 36–37.

CHAPTER 11

1. It was a little more complicated than that. To be specific, she suggested sitting cross-legged, hands held crossed over one another and in front of my heart, eyes closed. Then breathing in through my nose, out through my nose, in through my mouth with lips making an *o*, then out through my mouth with a gentle but audible sigh. And then a different pattern: in through my nose, out through my mouth, in through my mouth, out through my nose. I alternated those two breath patterns throughout the seven minutes.
2. Peter Wohlleben, *The Hidden Life of Trees: What They Feel, How They Communicate* (Vancouver, BC: Greystone Books, 2016), 81.
3. Jonathan Collins, Timothy Mackie, and Carissa Quinn, "The Most Quoted Verse in the Bible," August 17, 2020, in *BibleProject Podcast*, produced by Dan Gummel and Camden McAfee, podcast, MP3 audio, 56:00, https://bibleproject.com/podcast/most-quoted-verse-bible/.
4. Eli Saslow, "The White Flight of Derek Black," *Washington Post*, October 15, 2016, https://www.washingtonpost.com/national/the-white-flight-of-derek-black/2016/10/15/ed5f906a-8f3b-11e6-a6a3-d50061aa9fae_story.html.
5. Anthony Ray Hinton and Lara Love Hardin, *The Sun Does Shine: How I Found Life and Freedom on Death Row* (New York: St. Martin's Press, 2018), 170, chap. 17, Kindle.

CHAPTER 12

1. Ian Marcus Corbin, "Americans, Stop Being Ashamed of Weakness," *New York Times*, November 5, 2020, https://www.nytimes.com/2020/11/05/opinion/sunday/loneliness-weakness-america.html. Thank you to Liuan Huska for drawing my attention to this article.
2. Walter Brueggemann, *Living toward a Vision: Biblical Reflections on Shalom* (New York: United Church Press, 1982), 16.
3. Lisa Sharon Harper, *The Very Good Gospel: How Everything Wrong Can Be Made Right* (Colorado Springs: WaterBrook, 2016), 14.
4. Timothy Keller, "Justice in the Bible," Gospel in Life (Fall 2020), last modified October 16, 2020, https://quarterly.gospelinlife.com/justice-in-the-bible/.
5. Dominique Gilliard, *Rethinking Incarceration: Advocating for Justice That Restores* (Downers Grove, IL: InterVarsity Press, 2018), 139.
6. Gina Barton, "Community Plays a Role in Helping Ex-Prisoners," *Milwaukee Journal Sentinel* (May 15, 2016), https://www.postcrescent.com/story/news/2016/05/15/community-plays-role-helping-ex-prisoners/84409854/.
7. Rich Villodas, *The Deeply Formed Life: Five Transformative Values to Root Us* (Colorado Springs: WaterBrook Press, 2020), 59.

8. Gregory Boyle, *Tattoos on the Heart: The Power of Boundless Compassion* (New York: Free Press, 2010), 158, chap. 7, Kindle.

9. Martin Luther King Jr., *Strength to Love*, gift ed. (Minneapolis: Fortress Press, 2010), 30.

10. Terry Gross with Bryan Stevenson, "'Just Mercy' Attorney Asks U.S. To Reckon with Its Racist Past and Present," *NPR Fresh Air*, produced by Danny Miller, transcript, https://www.npr.org/transcripts/796234496. Used with permission.

CHAPTER 13

1. Makoto Fujimura, *Art and Faith: A Theology of Making* (New Haven, CT: Yale University Press, 2020), 46.

2. Henri J. Nouwen, *Life of the Beloved: Spiritual Living in a Secular World* (New York: Crossroad Publishing, 1992), 79.

3. These words are my own, but they have been heavily influenced by Erik Carter's work "Belonging," Erik W. Carter, accessed September 28, 2021, https://www.erikwcarter.com/belonging.

4. Skylar Mitchell, "Why I Chose a Historically Black College," *New York Times*, April 1, 2017, https://www.nytimes.com/2017/04/01/opinion/sunday/finding-growth-at-my-historically-black-college.html.

5. Story used with permission from David Bailey, director of Arrabon, a nonprofit that equips Christian leaders and their communities for the work of reconciliation.

EPILOGUE

1. Emmanuel Katongole and Chris Rice, *Reconciling All Things: A Christian Vision for Justice, Peace, and Healing* (Downers Grove, IL: IVP Books, 2008), 75–94.

The Author

Amy Julia Becker is an award-winning writer and speaker on faith, family, disability, and culture. She is the author of four books, including most recently *White Picket Fences: Turning toward Love in a World Divided by Privilege*. She hosts the *Love Is Stronger Than Fear* podcast.

Becker was born in Edenton, North Carolina, and has spent her adult life in the northeastern United States. A graduate of Princeton University and Princeton Theological Seminary, Becker now lives with her husband Peter and their three children, Penny, William, and Marilee, in western Connecticut. Becker has a bivocational license with the Evangelical Covenant Church. She and her family are members of Salem Covenant Church.

For more information and free resources, visit Amy JuliaBecker.com, where you can find downloadable resources, including *A Guide to Body Prayers*, *5 Ways to Receive God's Love and Practice Peace*, and *Head, Heart, and Hands*, a guide to participating in social healing.

OTHER BOOKS BY AMY JULIA BECKER

A Good and Perfect Gift: Faith, Expectations, and a Little Girl Named Penny

Small Talk: Learning from My Children about What Matters Most

White Picket Fences: Turning toward Love in a World Divided by Privilege